THE BELT AND ROAD INITIATIVE AS EPOCHAL REGIONALISATION

XIANGMING CHEN
with Julie Tian Miao and Xue Li

T0384043

Regional Studies Policy Impact Books
Series Editor: Philip R. Tomlinson

RSA **Regional Studies**
Association

Research Today, Policy Tomorrow

First published 2020
by Taylor & Francis
4 Park Square, Milton Park, Abingdon, Oxon, OX14 4RN

Taylor & Francis Group, an informa business

© 2020 Xiangming Chen

British Library Cataloguing-in-Publication Data
A catalogue record for this book is available from the British Library.

Trademark notice: Product or corporate names may be trademarks or registered trademarks, and are used only for identification and explanation without intent to infringe.

ISBN13: 978-0-367-70955-6 (print)
ISBN13: 978-1-003-14868-5 (e-book)

Typeset in 10.5/13.5 Univers LT Std
by Nova Techset Private Limited, Bengaluru and Chennai, India

Disclaimer
Every effort has been made to contact copyright holders for their permission to reprint material in this book. The publishers would be grateful to hear from any copyright holder who is not here acknowledged and will undertake to rectify any errors or omissions in future editions of this book.

CONTENTS

THE BELT AND ROAD INITIATIVE AS EPOCHAL REGIONALISATION

FOREWORD

For China, the Belt and Road Initiative (BRI) is part of a response to two questions: What is wrong with our world? What should we do about it?[1] As Xi Jinping has pointed out, global interdependence has increased and scientific and technological progress has been made. Indeed, the world is on the verge of a new industrial revolution. The world, however, also faces instability and great uncertainty. The world's economic growth is inadequate and uneven; the gap between the rich and the poor is getting worse; regional conflicts have emerged one after another; and there are major security threats associated with terrorism, cyber security and major infectious diseases. The arrival of a major zoonotic white swan even in the shape of COVID-19 and the powerful economic chain reactions that it catalysed and intensified indicated our vulnerabilities and the need to face common challenges jointly. Combined with other challenges such as climate change and its consequences that include the bush fires in Australia in late 2019 and the floods in China in early 2020, these events all point to the need to build a community with a shared future for mankind.

For China, the BRI is a call for a world order centred on cooperation, commerce and economic development under the guiding principle of no interference in the domestic affairs of sovereign states. At a macro-scale it is a multi-scalar *cooperation platform open to all countries* enabling them to couple national development strategies, harnessing comparative strengths and establishing strong complementarities. At the meso-scale, it aims to build jointly six land economic corridors and three maritime routes, although in recent years its geographical scope has widened to countenance a world land bridge. At the micro-scale, it involves a huge number of supporting nodes: major cities and industrial parks, medical centres, community learning centres and scientific and cultural institutions as this Policy Expo book illustrates so well.

The rise (return) of China and its decision to go out has, however, generated major concerns, especially in the United States and some Western countries. For Francis Fukuyama, the BRI is part of 'an historic

---

[1] Xi Jinping (2017) Building a community with a common future for humankind [人命运共同体]. Paper presented at the United Nations, Geneva, Switzerland, 18 January.

https://doi.org/10.1080/2578711X.2020.1822625

contest ... over competing development models ... between China ... and the United States (US) and other Western countries'. For French Finance Minister Bruno Le Maire: 'unless we ... reinvent Bretton Woods, the New Silk Roads might become the new world order ... and Chinese standards on state aid, on access to public procurement, on intellectual property could become the new global standards'. For Paul Wolfowitz, 'our first objective is to prevent the re-emergence of a new rival. ... We must maintain the mechanism for deterring potential competitors from even aspiring to a larger regional or global role'.[2]

In this situation the BRI has itself been a target of criticism from political leaders and the media in several largely Western countries. These criticisms have led to corrections including commitments to transparency, green development, enhanced consultation, sharing intellectual property and the establishment of dispute settlement mechanisms. It is also the case, however, that some of the criticisms are misplaced and others are contested: the claims about debt-trap diplomacy are a case in point.[3] Dealing with these issues requires, amongst other things, detailed studies of individual projects of the kind offered in this volume and for which it makes a very welcome contribution to existing studies of the BRI and its implications.

The financial resources that underpin the BRI are immense and the projects it funds will provide opportunities in a peaceful world to make a significant contribution to the development of cities and regions, the reduction of development disparities, and the improvement of livelihoods. The cases examined in this Policy Expo book point to some of these contributions of the BRI initiative and policy recommendations for enhancing them.

Michael Dunford
Visiting Research Fellow, Chinese Academy of Sciences
and Emeritus Professor Sussex
August 2020

---

[2] Fukuyama F (2016) Exporting the Chinese model. *Project Syndicate*, 12 January. Available online at: www.project-syndicate.org/onpoint/china-one-belt-one-road-strategy-by-francis-fukuyama-2016-01?barrier=accesspaylog/.
[3] Brautigam D (2020) A critical look at Chinese 'debt-trap diplomacy': the rise of a meme. *Area Development and Policy*, 5(1): 1-14.

 https://doi.org/10.1080/2578711X.2020.1822625

PREFACE

As we began the project for this RSA Policy Expo book in September 2018, China's Belt and Road Initiative (BRI), five years after its inauguration in 2013, was grabbing increasing attention from the international community. This heightened attention revolves around the BRI's massive geographical scope, strong state direction and, most importantly, controversies regarding benefits such as trade and infrastructure connections versus costs such as heavy debt and environmental impact for some developing countries. As we began writing this book in early 2020, the world's attention turned overwhelmingly to the spread and disruption of COVID-19, which brought the world to a halt and left massive health and economic destructions along and beyond its global paths.

The first half of 2020 gave us a timely opportunity to rethink the book's topic and focus, at least partially, which led us to incorporate selected unfolding evidence that not only supplements the content already in place, but also amplifies the larger arguments and policy recommendations. If the BRI has propelled China further into a central role in the global economy and an emerging leader for a 'new' globalisation, COVID-19 has revealed the world's heavy dependence on China-dominated global medical supply chains during an unprecedented health crisis. As China's early suppression of the virus and economic recovery allowed it to provide medical assistance to many other countries, we have added evidence on a 'pandemic diplomacy' to the BRI as China sent medical supplies to virus-stricken Europe and other growing cargo along the China–Europe Freight Train routes (chapter 2). While some marvel at the massive scale and height of skyscrapers dotting China's cities erected over the past four decades, COVID-19 brought into sharp relief the spatial clustering of infected cases and deaths in many of the world's largest and densest cities. On alert, we have referred to the timely addition of a new clinic with testing facilities in the new Borten city on Laos' northern border with China, built by a private Chinese company (chapter 3). By pushing millions of the poor back into poverty and exposing the severely underdeveloped healthcare in some least developed countries, COVID-19 has confirmed the multidimensional meanings of the United Nations' 2030 Sustainable Development Goals (SDGs), including poverty reduction and healthcare equity. We have added China's efforts not only to create manufacturing jobs but also to build or upgrade hospitals in African cities such as Addis Ababa, Ethiopia, to strengthen severely inadequate medical infrastructure in anticipation of a worsening virus outbreak (chapter 4).

https://doi.org/10.1080/2578711X.2020.1823701
© 2020 Xiangming Chen

While COVID-19 shed a critical spotlight on China's already strong global influence, it should not blind us to the fact that the BRI has already carved out several cross-border regional paths of uneven national and local impacts. This book aims to capture how the BRI allows China to have forged new global and regional connectivities and accelerated urbanisation and development through a trio of case studies. Upon examining the cases in chapters 2–4, we set forth policy recommendations for the pertinent players and stakeholders. At the end of the book, we reveal the intersections and convergence among these three focal areas of analysis and contend that our recommended policies can steer the BRI to evolve from a single initiative to a synergistic force and a global public good.

Xiangming Chen
Raether Distinguished Professor of Global Urban Studies and Sociology,
Trinity College and Visiting Professor, Fudan University
31 August 2020

https://doi.org/10.1080/2578711X.2020.1823701

AUTHORS

The RSA Policy Expo book was written and finalised by Professor Xiangming Chen (Founding Director, Center for Urban and Global Studies, Raether Distinguished Professor of Global Urban Studies and Sociology, Trinity College, Connecticut, USA; Guest Professor, School of Social Development and Public Policy, Fudan University, Shanghai, China). Dr Julie Tian Miao (Senior Lecturer, Property and Economic Development in the Melbourne School of Design, Faculty of Architecture, Building and Planning, Australia) and Dr Xue Li (Associate Professor, Department of Sociology, School of Social Development and Public Policy, Fudan University, Shanghai, China) gave feedback and editorial comments.

ACKNOWLEDGEMENTS

This study was supported by the Policy Expo 2018 grant from the Regional Studies Association (RSA), for which we are grateful. Chen acknowledges the Paul Raether Distinguished Professorship Fund at Trinity College for additional field research support. Chen also thanks the Henry Luce Foundation for an institutional grant to Trinity College and the Karen and David Thomas Urban China Endowment at Trinity College's Center for Urban and Global Studies for supporting its Silk Road summer program in 2018, which inspired the research that went into chapter 2 of this book. Earlier ideas and information in different parts of this book were presented at the Research Institute for the Two Oceans, Yunnan University of Finance and Economics, China, 28 December 2018; the Nordic Center for Asian Studies in Copenhagen, Denmark; the International Institute for Asian Studies in Leiden, Germany; a workshop at the Open University, UK; the Leibniz Institute for Research on Society and Space in Erkner, Germany; the Mercator Institute for China Studies in Berlin, Germany; the Polytechnic University of Turin and the University of Turin, Italy, October–November 2019; a World Bank conference in Tashkent, Uzbekistan, 27 January 2020; and at the School of Architecture and Planning at Shenzhen University, China, via Zoom, 17 April 2020. Feedback from these audiences was kindly acknowledged. Chen thanks Edmund Downie, Sally Hardy, Neil Lee, Zhigao Liu, Peter Rimmer, Tao Song, Curtis Stone, Phil Tomlinson and Sharon Zukin for varied support and helpful comments on earlier drafts; Shuyue Zhang at Trinity College for research assistance; a team working for the China–Europe Chang'an Line in Xi'an, China, Enbao Zhou in Borten, Laos, Zhiqiang Han in Shenzhen, and Yunqi Zhang in Dongguan, China, for providing research support and valuable information for chapters 2, 3 and 4, respectively, Andrzej Jakubowski for providing a base version of Figure 2.2, Jiashun Xue for editing Figures 2.2 and 2.3, and Michael Dunford, Zhigao Liu and Peter Rimmer for writing the foreword and endorsements for the book. The image of the Three Camels and a Train is from the Xi'an ITLP WeChat public platform, reproduced with permission. Finally, Chen thanks the publishing team at Taylor & Francis. The author is responsible for any remaining errors.[1]

---

[1] Chapter section 2.4 draws from Chen X (2020) A working paper on the China–Europe freight train.

This article has been corrected with minor changes. These changes do not impact the academic content of the article.

ABBREVIATIONS

ABC	Agricultural Bank of China
ADR	Addis Ababa–Djibouti Railway
AIIB	Asia Infrastructure Investment Bank
BESETO	Beijing–Seoul–Tokyo
BOC	Bank of China
BRI	Belt and Road Initiative
CBD	central business district
CCB	China Construction Bank
CDB	China Development Bank
CEFT	China–Europe Freight Train
CLR	China–Laos Railway
CMG	China Merchants Group
CPEC	China–Pakistan Economic Corridor
CREC	China Railway Group Ltd
DCS	Dual Circulation Strategy (China)
DIFTZ	Djibouti International Free Trade Zone
DMP	Doraleh Multipurpose Port (Djibouti)
DRC	Democratic Republic of Congo
DSR	Digital Silk Road
ECZ	Economic Cooperation Zone (Mohan–Borten, China–Laos)
EIZ	Eastern Industrial Zone (Ethiopia)
ETDZ	Economic and Technology Development Zone
EximBank	Export–Import Bank (China)

FDI	foreign director investment
FTZ	free-trade zone
GDP	gross domestic product
GPG	global public good
ICBC	Industrial and Commercial Bank of China
ITLP	International Trade and Logistics Park (Xi'an, China)
LG	location quotient
MDG	Millennium Development Goal (United Nations)
MOU	memorandum of understanding
NDB	National Development Bank (China)
OECD	Organisation for Economic Co-operation and Development
OTECZ	Overseas Trade and Economic Cooperation Zone (China–Africa)
PPC	port–park–city
RPG	regional public good
SDG	Sustainable Development Goal (United Nations)
SDZ	Saysettha Development Zone (Vientiane, Laos)
SEZ	special economic zone
SOE	state-owned enterprise
SRF	Silk Road Fund (China)
SWF	sovereign wealth fund
UNCTAD	United Nations Conference on Trade and Development

https://doi.org/10.1080/2578711X.2020.1823709

EXECUTIVE SUMMARY

COVID-19 is a rare historic event with world-altering consequences. China's Belt and Road Initiative (BRI) is an epochal initiative with more moving parts and a longer time horizon that is capable of changing the world on a more lasting basis than the shorter term disruption of the coronavirus pandemic. The BRI's epochal significance and impact reside in its multifaceted regionalisation through the creation of six growth corridors of varied length. These corridors, which also comprise several other shorter sub-corridors, mark an unprecedented era of new large-scale regional development and transformation with wide and deep global, national and local consequences.

First, these BRI-induced corridors originate from deep inside China's uneven domestic regional development. They were extended outward from China's geographical turn toward its Western region around the year 2000 in response to the enlarged regional disparity resulting from its earlier turn toward its coastal region in 1980. Second, these corridors traverse a large number of neighbouring countries, cross many international borders, touch and pass numerous remote and marginal cities and towns, and forge a myriad of new intra- and cross-regional connections between China and a vast swath of the world.

Given their large scale, far reach and layered composition, these regional corridors affect the master processes of globalisation, urbanisation and development (see Box 1). This Regional Studies Association

---

Box 1   The BRI's impacts on globalisation, urbanisation and development:

- The BRI has influenced globalisation by forging new cross-border connections and channels for trade such as the China–Europe Freight Train (CEFT) between western China and Europe through Eurasia (chapter 2)
- The BRI has influenced urbanisation beyond China through China-built new cities and transport corridors by linking them to other cities and hinterlands such as Borten on the China–Laos border and the China–Laos Railway (CLR) (chapter 3)
- The BRI has affected development in faraway lands through China-built special economic zones that function as sustainable anchors for local and national industrialisation as in Djibouti and Ethiopia(chapter 4)

---

https://doi.org/10.1080/2578711X.2020.1823708
© 2020 Xiangming Chen

(RSA) Policy Expo book observes these impacts at multiple scales, from redirected trade flows between China and some countries west of China to China-built new cities, economic zones and transport systems within and across a variety of other countries in Asia and Africa. In addition, we have uncovered three connected mechanisms – connectivity, infrastructure and sustainability – that deliver and transmit the BRI's impact onto globalisation, urbanisation and development, respectively (chapter 1):

This book documents the parallel development between a major BRI corridor and the China–Europe Freight Train (CEFT) (chapter 2). This combination of a cross-border corridor and multiple freight train routes along it in turn benefited from both a reimagination of the historic Silk Road trade route and a reincarnation of the exiting Eurasian land bridge. Despite its short existence, the CEFT has blossomed into an expanded number of new freight routes linking a large number of cities in China, Central Asia and Europe. While relatively recent, the CEFT has proven its resilience and longer term sustainability. Against the disruption caused by COVID-19, the CEFT ran 3953 trains which carried 356,000 containers of traded goods in both directions between 1 January and 30 May 2020, up 28% and 32% from the same period in 2019 (chapter 2).

Our analysis traces the BRI's inside-out impact on global urbanisation from China's own unprecedentedly rapid and massive city-building to its growing role in constructing new cities and associated urban and transport infrastructures in its neighbouring countries and distant lands. Through a paired analysis of Borten as a China-built new border city and the China–Laos Railway (CLR), we have demonstrated how one BRI corridor has channelled China's external power in accelerating overseas urban development, often partly in its own approach, form and function (chapter 3). We have also examined how a segment of China's Maritime Silk Road – a sort of ocean corridor – has unleashed economic development in Djibouti and Ethiopia through both port upgrading and special zone-based industrialisation, as well as a new cross-national freight train connection (chapter 4). We reveal the separate but simultaneous participation of powerful state enterprises and large private companies in driving sustainable development in Africa through forging new sea–land and inter-city economic ties and a more integrated approach to enhancing local economic and social development and welfare.

We have advanced polity recommendations at the end of chapters 2–4 and summarised the essential ones in Box 2.

Box 2   Policy recommendations for mutually beneficial interactions between the BRI and globalisation, urbanisation and development (a schematic summary):

- To turn the BRI from a China-driven initiative into a potential global public good, we need policies to promote efforts by all players and stakeholders at all government levels and in relevant economic sectors to work with the BRI-created connectivities in promoting trade, investment and other areas of cooperation
- In response to the BRI's impact on global urbanisation, we encourage urbanising developing countries to adopt policies to strengthen the coordination between central and local governments, initiate more realistic planning, enforce environmental standards, and reduce core-periphery spatial disparity

---

   https://doi.org/10.1080/2578711X.2020.1823708

- To enhance the BRI's positive impact on development, we advocate the development community of donors and other stakeholders to better align the United Nations's Sustainable Development Goals (SDGs) and the BRI, address the debt trap and debt relief, scale up China's labour-intensive manufacturing relocation, foster indigenous suppliers, promote skill development, and integrate economic development with broader social development

Finally, we reiterate that the BRI's impacts on globalisation, urbanisation and development have occurred through a series of ground-breaking regional corridors ushering in an era of epochal regionalism (chapter 5). We discuss how our recommended policies can help turn the BRI from a single initiative into a synergistic force that can contribute to the interconnected world as a global public good.

1. THE BRI AND REGIONALISATION

1.1 INTRODUCTION

Since China announced the Belt and Road Initiative (BRI) in 2013, the world's reaction to the BRI has remained mixed and even polarised about its intended benefits versus its real or potential costs. The BRI has generated some benefits through a variety of completed large-scale infrastructure projects in many countries and cities, while its costs include potential heavy debts and environmental externalities in developing countries that host some infrastructure projects. Regardless, the increasing global interest in the BRI is reflected in the fact that, by May 2020, 138 countries and 30 international organisations had signed around 200 BRI-related cooperation agreements with China.[1] This global interest is not surprising. The BRI geographically touches around 70 countries, including China, that contain about 60% of the world's population. In economic terms, according to the Chinese government's information, the BRI countries account for approximately one-third of the world's gross domestic product (GDP) and trade.[2]

Moving beyond a simple and static global perspective, we see the BRI as marking an epochal era of new regionalism and thus a momentous moment in history for understanding global, national and local processes today and in the future. In this book we focus on how the BRI is affecting three master processes – globalisation, urbanisation and development – by examining both the opportunities and the risks at the interface between the BRI and each process. As a more important purpose of this book, we aim to draw policy recommendations that can help turn the BRI from a China-driven initiative into a synergistic force working for global public goods.

The BRI's global significance appears to have drawn more attention from the government and business sectors than from the scholarly community. By a rough count, the BRI has been the focus of around 40 reports, many quite lengthy, by a variety of organisations. These include: key government agencies such as the National Development Bank (NDB) of China, prominent international development agencies such as the World Bank, United Nations and the OECD, think tanks such as the Brookings Institution, RAND Corporation and the Asia Society Policy Institute, and business consultancies such as McKinsey, Deloitte and Cushman & Wakefield. While these reports provide rich information, they lack a conceptually and analytically rigorous framework, which limits the range and adequacy of their recommended policies.

In the meantime, academic research on the BRI is catching up with a growing body of published work. Confronting this research community is the critical question of how to assess the scope and depth of the BRI's short- and long-term global impacts as its implementation proceeds. While scholars approach this question from varied assumptions and disciplinary perspectives, they have converged on adopting

---

[1] See www.yidaiyilu.gov.cn [Accessed 8 September 2020]. Available online at: https://mp.weixin.qq.com/s/BZ5vkU8lj3trJRRg3e7Jnw/.

[2] Cushman & Wakefield (2018) *Silk Road Rebirth, A Special Report*. Hong Kong: Cushman & Wakefield.

https://doi.org/10.1080/2578711X.2020.1823710

a macroscopic focus on the BRI as a state-directed geopolitical and geocultural strategy for advancing China's interests globally that draws from a reimagined connection to the ancient Silk Road.[3]

This prevailing view has been challenged by a few scholars who view the BRI as a loose scheme that has brought together diverse domestic interests and actors in China who interpret top-level policies differently and compete against each other.[4] In a similar vein, some see the BRI as driven by economic imperatives as opposed to geopolitical motives and by a fragmented and often bilateral approach instead of a singularly state-coordinated strategy.[5] The diversity of actors includes international, national and local policy-makers in and out of China who try to understand the scope and strength of the BRI's impact. In this policy-facing book, we adopt a new region-centric approach to demonstrating how the BRI has affected globalisation, urbanisation and development within and across a variety of countries and cities and advance appropriate policy recommendations. In doing so, we highlight and accentuate place-specific processes and outcomes triggered and shaped by the BRI's regional corridors as they have taken place and form and stretch out. This approach takes the reader from the high and somewhat abstract global and inter-state views on the BRI all the way down to the ground level where some places and peoples across the three continents of Europe, Asia and Africa have been altered through becoming connected to and part of the BRI's cross-border regional corridors.

In the remainder of this introductory chapter, we highlight the significant features of the BRI as a new form of global regionalism whose geographical scope and economic impact may be unprecedented. We propose a framework for understanding the BRI as epochal regionalism and its strong and wide-ranging impacts on globalisation, urbanisation and development. The next three chapters discuss how the BRI affects globalisation, urbanisation and development respectively through three case studies. They focus on: 1) continental freight train routes across Eurasia; 2) the pairing of a boundary-spanning new city and new railway between China and mainland Southeast Asia; and 3) a multidimensional nexus of a new seaport, a new bi-national railway and recent special zone-based export-oriented industrialization in Eastern Africa.

In chapter 2, we argue that the BRI can usher in a new era of China-led globalisation. Led by Western advanced countries, especially the United States, and their large multinational corporations and banks, globalisation thus far features interconnected supply chains, highly developed financial services and the increasing dominance of digital technology that favours a small number of leaders and drivers and disadvantage many less and least developing countries. This West-led globalisation has produced large inequalities between rich and poor countries and persistently lagged development for some of the latter. As the world's

---

[3] Recent book-length studies include: Griffiths R (2017) *Revitalizing the Silk Road: China's Belt and Road Initiative*. Leiden: Hipe; Maçães B (2018) *Belt and Road: A Chinese World Order*. London: Hurst; Winter T (2019) *Geocultural Power: China's Quest to Revive the Silk Roads for the Twenty-First Century*. Chicago: University of Chicago Book; and Li X (ed.) (2019) *Mapping China's 'One Belt One Road' Initiative*. London: Palgrave Macmillan.

[4] Jones L and Zeng J (2019) Understanding China's 'Belt and Road Initiative': Beyond 'grand strategy' to a state transformation analysis. *Third World Quarterly*, 40(8): 1415–1439.

[5] Jones L and Hameiri S (2020) *Debunking the Myth of 'Debt-Trap Diplomacy': How Recipient Countries Shape China's Belt and Road Initiative*. Research Paper, August. London: Chatham House.

second largest economy but still a partly developing country, China has begun to drive a new globalisation by making many new cross-border connections through large-scale infrastructure construction, primarily in developing countries. Policy-makers may wonder about what this China-led globalisation means and how it affects the world. We set out to make sense of both China-led globalisation and its policy implications.

In chapter 3, we examine how the BRI can produce new pathways for faster and connected urbanisation in developing countries that extend from the Chinese experience. Using China-built ports and industrial zones in Southeast Asia, we scrutinise the early stages of sequential urban development in these countries that bears the imprint of China's own urbanisation. In addition, as the BRI has generated opportunities for smaller and peripheral cities to become important nodal points on and along cross-border growth corridors, we draw lessons and implications for understanding, anticipating and responding to a new stage of China-fuelled urbanisation in the developing world.

In chapter 4, we investigate how the BRI is capable of creating new development opportunities and risks that reflect the Chinese context and experience and their projection overseas. Seeing the BRI as extending a China-style development strategy, we focus on whether state policies to induce market practices such as the use of special economic zones (SEZs) at the local level can transfer successfully to other institutional contexts. We highlight opportunities for using certain mechanisms to adapt the Chinese approach to such African developing nations as Djibouti and Ethiopia, while identifying the risks that hamper the indigenous replication of China's development success. This allows us to address the question of whether China-inspired development is sustainable in other developing countries where conditions are somewhat or vastly different.

These chapters end with respective sets of policy recommendations based on the case analyses for policy-makers concerned about China's growing impacts on globalisation, urbanisation and development. The last chapter brings the connected threads together to show that good and fitting policies can guide the BRI from a single initiative to a synergistic force. We reserve the final word for discussing the potential for the BRI to become a global public good in the long run.

1.2 THE BRI AS NEW REGIONALISATION

The BRI combines an overland 'belt' linking China to Europe through Central Asia, and a maritime 'road' leading from China to Europe via Southeast Asia, the Gulf region and Eastern Africa. More specifically, the BRI comprises of six mostly overland economic corridors (Figure 1.1 and Box 1.1).

While we know the approximate ends of these corridors, it is difficult to specify their exact length and width, and thereby scope. These corridors share two salient features. They are not only elongated regions but also span multiple countries and slice international borders. In addition, these six corridors encompass around 30 other sub-corridors or corridor projects.[6] Corridor 4, for example, includes both the China–Laos

---

[6] Rimmer P (2020) *China's Global Vision and Actions: Reactions to Belt, Road and Beyond*. Cheltenham: Edward Elgar.

 https://doi.org/10.1080/2578711X.2020.1823710

Figure 1.1 The Belt and Road Initiative's (BRI) six (regional) corridors

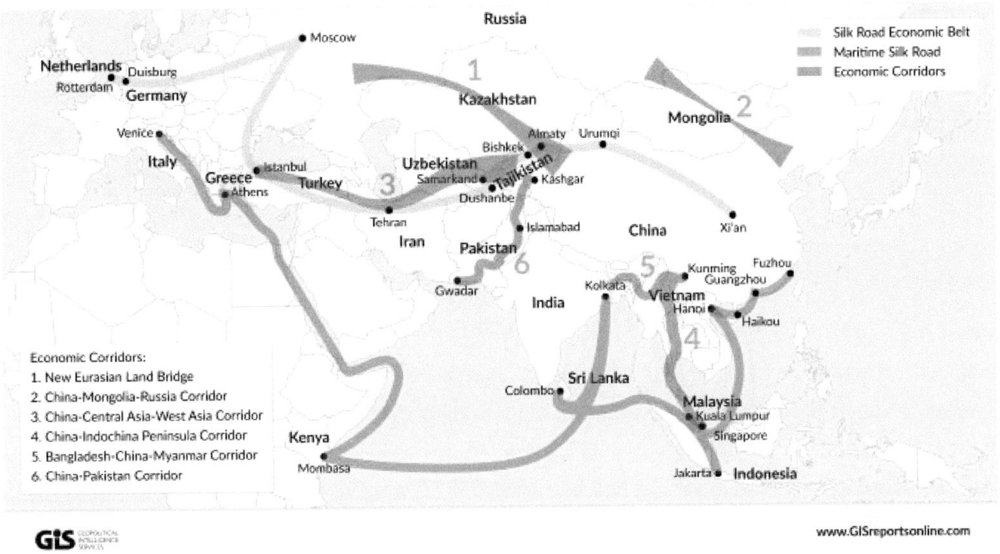

Source: GISreportsonline.com. Available online at: www.gisreportsonline.com/gis-dossier-chinas-belt-and-road-initiative,politics,2608.html/

> **Box 1.1 The BRI's six overland growth corridors:**
>
> - The New Eurasian Land Bridge Corridor
> - The China–Mongolia–Russia Corridor
> - The China–Central Asia–West Asia Economic Corridor
> - The China–Indochina Peninsular Corridor
> - The Bangladesh–China–India–Myanmar Corridor
> - The China–Pakistan Economic Corridor

and China–Myanmar economic corridors. The combination of long corridor shape, large territorial coverage and complex spatial composition distinguishes the BRI's six corridors as a new form of regionalisation with strong global significance and impact across multiple spatial scales. Regionalisation is not the opposite trend against globalisation. It not only scales up to but also reinforces globalisation, as we demonstrate in chapter 2.

Regional corridors are far from new to the BRI today. They share an age-old connection going back to the Silk Road of corridor-shaped route(s) linking the ancient Chinese city of Xi'an through Dunhuang (Gansu province) and Kashgar (Xinjiang) to Tashkent (Uzbekistan) through Eurasia and beyond. This long-standing connection provided the foundational rationale for the belt in the BRI. Corridors that are more recent have formed across North America, Europe and Asia. From the late 1950s, the Northeastern corridor of the United States began to form linking Boston and Washington DC through the New York metropolitan area into the so-called 'Bos-Wash' megalopolis. It has been a suburbanised agglomeration with complex patterns of class, education, housing, race and ethnicity. In Europe, the so-called 'Blue Banana' extends south from Manchester through London in south-east England, northern France, the Benelux countries and ends at Milan in northern Italy. It features regionalised historical and commercial ties between geographical neighbours as borders gradually lost their barrier effects through the establishment of the European Union in 1993 and of the Schengen agreement in 1995. Of the multiple urban corridors in Asia, the so-called 'BESETO' corridor stretches from Beijing to Seoul via Tokyo. It features a combined population of over 100 million people and over 100 smaller cities over sea and land international borders that began to take shape from the 1980s.[7]

Despite their different histories and geographies, these prominent urban and regional corridors share the salient attributes of being market induced with no or little formal inter-city coordination. They are anchored to major national and international hubs in developed economies with uneven numbers of intra-corridor spatial gaps. Among a large number of urban corridors, three ranked in the top few in geographical length and covered area. The Bos-Wash ran 950 km and covered 142,452 km^2, the Blue Banana 2300 km and 444,883 km^2, and the BESETO 2900 km and 196,244 km^2.[8] In comparison, the BRI corridors are initiated by the Chinese state, contain a greater variety of less developed countries and cities, and a much larger number of gaps separating longer distances. Two of the shorter BRI corridors, however, are of comparable length. The China–Pakistan Economic Corridor (CPEC) runs about 2000 km from the Pakistani port of Gwadar to Kashgar in Xinjiang, China, while the China–Indochina Peninsula Economic Corridor covers about 2600 km, with the Chinese city of Kunming and the country of Singapore as the anchors at both ends. With the Chinese state as the driver, the longer and larger territorial coverage, more borders, and the blending of diverse and unevenly developed cities, the BRI corridors constitute a collection of elongated regions that mark a new era of large-scale regionalisation with a wide range of global and local impacts.

The BRI's economic scope and weight relative to that of the world's are wide and heavy because China is the world's second largest economy and its largest trading nation. China's share of the world's GDP has surged since 1980 to 18.7%, while its share of the world's trade has surged four-fold since 1980 (Box 1.2).[9] China effectively accounts for half the BRI countries' total GDP and more than one-third of their trade. Even with China, the original 65 BRI countries' share of the world's GDP grew to only 30% in 2017 from lower levels

> **Box 1.2 China's shares of the world's gross domestic product (GDP): 3.0% in 1980 and 18.7% in 2018.**
>
> **China's share of the world's trade: 3.0% in 1995 and 12.4% in 2018**

---

[7] Choe S-C (1997) The evolving urban system in North-East Asia. In Lo F-C and Yeung Y-M (eds.), *Emerging World Cities in Pacific Asia*. Tokyo: United Nations University Press.

[8] Georg I, Blaschke T and Taubenböck H (2016) A global inventory of urban corridors based on perceptions and nighttime light imagery. *ISPRS International Journal of Geo-Information*, 5(233): 2–19. doi:10.3390/ijgi5120233.

[9] Center for Strategic and International Studies (CSIS) (2019) *ChinaPower*. Available online at: https://chinapower.csis.org/trade-partner/.

https://doi.org/10.1080/2578711X.2020.1823710

(Figure 1.2). While GDP per capita for the 65 BRI countries grew steadily over the same period, driven largely by China, it remained at 48.9% of the world's average in 2017 (Figure 1.3). This suggests that China is capable of driving growth in the less developed BRI countries by generating more trade and investment.

In 2013 when the BRI was launched, the BRI countries accounted for 25.0% of China's total trade. This figure rose went up to 26.5% in 2017. China's imports from the BRI countries rose 12.1%, while its exports

Figure 1.2   Global gross domestic product (GDP) versus the GDP for 65 BRI countries

US$Trillion

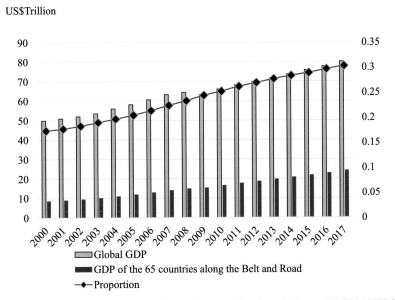

Source: Compiled from the World Bank online data at https://data.worldbank.org/indicator/NY.GDP.MKTP.CD.

Figure 1.3   World's gross domestic product (GDP) per capita versus GDP for 65 BRI countries per capita

US$

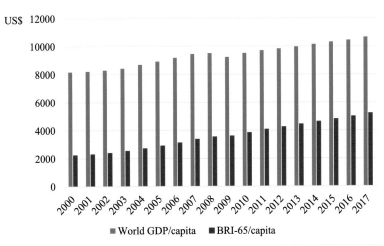

Source: Compiled from the World Bank online data at https://data.worldbank.org/indicator/NY.GDP.MKTP.CD.

to the BRI countries dropped 3.9% between 2013 and 2017.[10] More recent data show that cumulative total trade between China and BRI countries reached US$7.8 trillion during 2013–19, with an average annual growth of over 6%.[11] China's trade with BRI countries totalled US$1.34 trillion in 2019 (US$762.3 billion for China's exports and US$581.7 billion for China's imports), up 10.8% year on year, outpacing China's aggregate trade growth by 7.4%. The BRI countries' share of China's total trade approached 30% in 2019, up 2 percentage points from 2018. China has become the biggest trade partner for 25 BRI countries.[12]

China's investment into the BRI falls into four channels: policy banks, state-owned banks, sovereign wealth funds (SWFs) and international financing institutions (Box 1.3). The two policy banks – China Development Bank (CDB) and Export and Import Bank of China (EximBank) – are the largest direct sources of funding for the BRI. The four state-owned banks – Industrial and Commercial Bank of China (ICBC), China Construction Bank (CCB), Agricultural Bank of China (ABC) and Bank of China (BOC) – contribute to BRI funding by financing domestic projects primarily. The SWFs such as the Silk Road Fund (SRF), which invest in bonds, precious metals and real estate, get involved in funding BRI projects around the world. The fourth channel includes institutions such as the 56-member Asian Infrastructure Investment Bank (AIIB), which has invested in projects in emerging Asia through the BRI.[13] These institutions bring together the Chinese state's strategic and strong financing capacity and put it behind the BRI.

According to one generous projection, the BRI may call for an estimated US$4–8 trillion over time, without a clearly specified end date for completion.[14] Just for the 10-year period from 2017, BRI investment projects are estimated to add over US$1 trillion of outward funding for foreign infrastructure.[15] This makes the BRI the world's largest and most costly initiative in history. From 2013 to 2019, China's cumulative BRI investment reached approximately US$180 billion, which accounted for 8.2% of the stock of China's total FDI to date. Figure 1.4 shows the annual flows of China's investment into the BRI countries. While fluctuating from year to year, this investment flow reached US$18.7 billion and 13.7% of China's total FDI flows in 2019, up from 11.7% in 2013 and 12% in 2017. By a broader measure, during 2013–18, the combination of BRI investment and construction contracts totalled US$614 billion, accounting for 53% of the value of all such transactions by China globally and 61% of the number of such contracts.[16] Without data on the shares of

[10] Weidong Liu et al. (2019) *A Third-Party Appraisal of the BRI Progress 2013–2018.* Beijing: Commercial Publishing House.

[11] See www.yidaiyilu.gov.cn; see Reference 1.

[12] Xinhua (2020) *China's Trade with BRI Countries Booms in 2019.* Available online at: www.xinhuanet.com/english/2020-01/14/c_138704581.htm [Accessed 14 January 2020].

[13] Financing and funding for the Belt & Road Initiative. *Belt & Road News*, 17 May. Available online at: https://www.beltandroad.news/2019/05/17/financing-and-funding-for-the-belt-road-initiative/.

[14] See https://www.beltroad-initiative.com/belt-and-road/.

[15] Organisation for Economic Co-operation and Development (OECD) (2018) *China's Belt and Road Initiative in the Global Trade, Investment and Finance Landscape.* OECD Business and Financial Outlook 2018. Paris: OECD. Available online at: www.oecd.org/daf/.

[16] China Global Investment Tracker, The American Enterprise and Investment Institute and The Heritage Foundation, cited by Moody's Analytics, June 2019.

Figure 1.4   China's annual investment flows into BRI countries, 2013–19

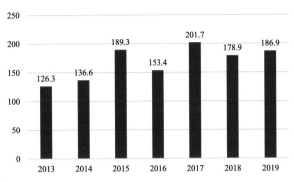

Note: Hundred million US$
Source: *The Statistical Report on China's Foreign Direct Investment 2019*. Available online at: https://mp.weixin.qq.com/s/
y6Yz4_nShjPdfWbUV9y_aw

funding from the four channels (Box 1.3), we have found that the EximBank provided more than US$149 billion to more than 1800 BRI projects through 2018, while the CDB provided financing in excess of US$190 billion for more than 600 BRI projects.[17]

In addition, Chinese enterprises invested over US$90 billion directly in the BRI countries, with an average annual increase of 5.2% during the period 2013–18. The contract value of newly signed overseas projects in these countries registered over US$600 billion, representing an average annual increase

> **Box 1.3   Four official channels of China's investment into the BRI**
>
> - Policy banks
> - State-owned banks
> - Sovereign wealth funds
> - International financing institutions

of 11.9%,[18] although state-sponsored BRI investment has slowed since the second BRI Forum in April 2019 and the outbreak of the COVID-19 pandemic in early 2020. However, China's state and private companies form the sources of the BRI's investment beyond the four official channels (Box 1.3). We show how these companies work with China's national and provincial governments in executing BRI projects (see chapters 2–4).

Besides accounting for a growing share of China's trade against the slowdown in overall global trade (chapter 2), the BRI absorbed a massive amount of Chinese outward investment through a variety of public and private financing channels. An increased volume of this investment has been attributed to and claimed by the BRI since 2013 that otherwise might not have left China without the BRI. Some of China's overseas projects that started right before or around 2013 were retrospectively added into the BRI's total financing

---

[17]Weidong Liu et al. (2019); see Reference 10.
[18]Ministry of Foreign Affairs (2019) *China's Progress Report on Implementation of the 2030 Agenda for Sustainable Development*. Beijing: Ministry of Foreign Affairs.

(see chapters 2–4). To the extent the BRI has generated a substantial amount of China's foreign trade and investment, its worldwide influence becomes more meaningful if viewed through a regional lens on China's domestic economic and spatial transformations.

1.3 THE BRI FROM CHINA'S REGIONAL PERSPECTIVE

While the BRI is often seen as China's external strategy for gaining global influence, we temper this view by (re)locating the BRI, especially its motivating conditions and feedback consequences, deep inside China's diverse domestic regional spaces. The spatial transformation of China's economy over the past four decades has many dimensions. To connect this transformation clearly to the BRI, we recast it as China's two historic turns that have created the dynamic context for understanding the BRI's corridor-centric regional forms and impacts (Table 1.1).

China made its first historic turn to its coastal or eastern region around 1980, marked by the opening of four SEZs in 1979 on its south-eastern shore and the economic and technological development zones (ETDZs) in 14 other coastal cities including Shanghai in 1984. That was when East Asian economies such as Hong Kong, Taiwan, Korea and Japan were looking to relocate their labour-intensive industries. China's coastal

Table 1.1   China's two historic regional turns, around 1980 versus 2000:

West (Eurasia)	Inland (West)	Coastal (East)	East (Asia-Pacific)
• Limited trade • Lower priority • Less political stability • Greater ethnic diversity • Border barriers	• Neglected investment • Lagging development • Origins of out-migration • Supply of raw materials	• Favoured investment • Faster development • Greater prosperity • Destinations of in-migration • Strong global integration	• Sources of capital investment • Trade partners • Export markets • Cultural similarity
		⟶ ⟶	*First turn*
• Targets of investment • Sites for new infrastructure projects • Connective points	• Infused investment • Faster growth • Return migration • Growing global connections	• Source of investment • Manufacturing relocation • Provider of poverty alleviation	
Second turn ⟵	⟵ ⟵		
**Eurasia (Europe, Central Asia, South Asia and West Asia) benefits from China's 'Go West' and Belt and Road Initiative (BRI) by obtaining heavy Chinese investment	**The inland region lost out and fell behind during the first turn, but it gains from catch-up development during the second turn	*The coastal region benefited from favourable policies such as special economic zones (SEZs) during the first turn and contributed to interior development during the second turn	*East Asian economies (Hong Kong, Taiwan, Korea and Japan) helped China's coastal region prosper and globally integrate

Source: Lead author.

Note: The first row denotes China's first double and eastward turn to its coastal region domestically and to the East Asian economies in the late 1970s and early 1980s. The second row characterises China's second and westward turn to its inland and border regions domestically and to Eurasia and Europe internationally in the late 1990s and early 2000s. Source: Lead author.

cities with special zones were endowed with favourable locations, seaports and other better infrastructure facilities. Opening and reform favouring a small number of areas, even if they were to fail, would be geographically and institutionally restricted.

The first turn was very successful. The most important indicator of this success was the concentration of foreign direct investment (FDI) in China. From 1978 to 1998, cumulatively 85% of foreign investment flowed into China's coastal areas, while only 3% was in the western or inland region.[19] This uneven spatial distribution undergirded the growing stock of FDI in China to over US$300 billion at the end of 1999, making China the largest FDI recipient among all developing nations. As a result, China's share of global trade trebled from 1% in 1980 to more than 3% in 1999.[20] This reflects the dominant role of FDI in China's international trade, weighted heavily to exports, as foreign-invested enterprises accounted for nearly half of China's exports in 1996, a leap from 1% in 1985.

The coast-oriented or eastward turn led to considerable gain in economic dynamism and efficiency at the expense of balanced development and spatial equity (Figure 1.4). While the central region increased its FDI share from 1.1% in 1983 to 8.8% in 1993 through policy extension and new investment, the western region's share dropped from 5.9% to 3.7% and further to 0.5% by 1997, despite having over 50% of China's land and 20% of its population. The location quotient (LQ)[21] for income per capita for China's western region, relative to the national average of 100, fell from 70 in 1978 to 68 in 1992 and then to 63 in 1997. In the opposite direction, the LQ for the eastern region rose from 129 in 1978 to 136 in 1992 and to 148 in 1997.[22] This interregional inequality challenged balanced development and political stability.

In response, the Chinese government introduced a growing set of policies from 1992 that ultimately amounted to the historic second turn of development strategy to the inland and western region. In 1992, all the capital cities of inland provinces, 13 border cities and 10 interior cities along the Yangtze River were granted favourable FDI policies such as lower taxes and faster approval of projects that had been confined to coastal cities. The turn to the interior and west was accelerated in 1997 when the central government granted the status of central government municipality to Chongqing designating this megacity as a central hub for the Western region. It was not until 2000 that China's second historic turn to the inland took hold through the official launch of the 'Go West' policy. It led to the establishment of 17 new ETDZs, most of which located in the west during 2000–02. While the Go West policy constituted the domestic side of China's second turn, the 'Go Global' policy, officially launched in 1999, was the complementary

---

[19] Cheng S (2006) From East to West: The evolution of China's FDI preferential policies. *Journal of the Washington Institute of China Studies*, 1(1): 60–77.

[20] Lemoine F (2000) *FDI and the Opening Up of China's Economy*. Working Paper No. 2000, 11 June. CEPII Research and Expertise on the World Economy (Recherche et Expertise sur L'Economie Mondiale). Paris: Centre d'Études Prospectives et d'Informations Internationales (CEPII).

[21] Location quotient (LQ) is a measure of the degree of concentration of a particular industry or region relative to the national average.

[22] Hao, F H and Wei Y D (2016) *Regional Inequality in China: Trends, Scales and Mechanisms*. Working Paper Series No. 202. Santiago: Rimisp.

international wing of the second turn. This pair of policies laid the logical and geographical foundation for China's BRI in 2013 to emerge as the culmination of the second turn (Box 1.4).[23]

The second turn around the year 2000 came about exactly at the halfway point of China's four decades of domestic transformation and global integration. The two turns feature opposite geographical directions with the first turn toward and focused on China's coastal region, and the second oriented and fixated on its western region. While the first turn aimed at connecting China to the global economy using the sea, the second turn is focused on building overland connections with countries bordering China's western frontier, including landlocked economies in Central Asia. The first turn focused on export-oriented manufacturing and led to the creation and consolidation of agglomerated and regionalised manufacturing hubs and their supply chains. The second turn, however, has favoured infrastructure-oriented development capable of reshaping the coast-dominated national manufacturing landscape and creating more benefits for the much less developed interior and western border regions (Table 1.1).

By announcing the new 'dual circulation' strategy (DCS) in May 2020, China may be entering a 'third turn' as a strategic response to the volatile and hostile global economic and geopolitical environment shaped by the pandemic and the United States' anti-China campaign. The DCS aims to rebalance away from its global exposure and integration as embodied and accelerated by the BRI by increasing and relying more on domestic consumption and internally integrated production and supply chains. Given the powerful domestic anchor and push for the BRI, the DCS can augment and refine the BRI's inside-out logic and extension by creating richer and stronger domestic opportunities that may lead to more targeted and sustainable overseas projects. This new development should refocus global attention on the outward regional impacts already generated by the BRI through China's two geographical turns and the BRI's regionally oriented corridors.

1.4 HOW TO UNPACK THE BRI'S REGIONAL IMPACTS

China's two geographical turns have provided the domestic regional source for the BRI's transnational regional orientation, trajectory and influence. Moreover, the two turns have shaped the origins and directions of the BRI corridors that link China's west and south-west regions into elongated cross-border paths of economic cooperation and development. We now propose a framework for understanding and analysing how the BRI exerts economic and spatial impacts on globalisation, urbanisation and development through its growth corridors as regional tentacles and channels (Figure 1.5).

---

[23]Chen X (2018) Globalization redux: Can China's inside-out strategy catalyze economic development across its Asian borderlands and beyond? *Cambridge Journal of Regions, Economy and Society*, 11(1): 35–58.

https://doi.org/10.1080/2578711X.2020.1823710

Figure 1.5 Framework for analysing the BRI

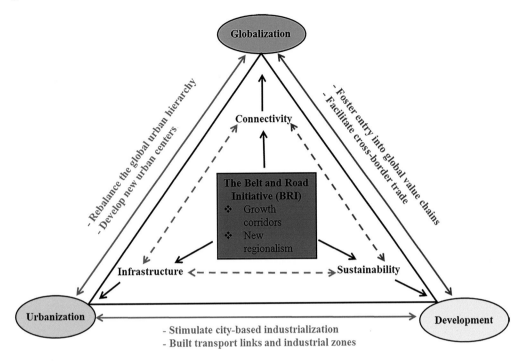

Source: Lead author

As Figure 1.5 suggests, we see the BRI as capable of affecting globalisation, urbanisation and development, respectively, through the regional conduits of corridors. We contend that the BRI exerts this three-fold impact through different but connected mechanisms. At the grandest scale, the BRI is capable of reshaping the current course and impact of globalisation as its six growth corridors weave and spin new spatial and material connections for increasing greater cross-border trade and investment flows. While globalisation has created greater economic integration, it has done so primarily through the connective power of financial flows and digital technology. This has benefited the dominant global cities more at the expense of smaller and geographically marginal places. The BRI has begun to create more trade and infrastructure connections among the cities and regions left behind by globalisation as led by the West over the past decades (see chapter 2).

From its impact on globalisation, the frameworks pivots to the BRI's parallel effect on global urbanisation, which can benefit from badly needed transport, industrial and municipal infrastructures financed and delivered along the growth corridors. Since the infrastructure complex is critical to but lags behind rapid global urbanisation, the BRI can accelerate and rebalance urbanisation by adding new infrastructure in cities of lagging regions. This causal connection rotates logically to the third leg of the framework, which points to the BRI's role in fostering economic development through faster industrialisation from infrastructure-fuelled urbanisation. The urbanisation–development nexus guides us to a deeper analysis of how new development can be sustainable when stimulated by China-provided infrastructure such as industrial zones and transport projects through the BRI. Economic development aided by the BRI in turn can facilitate more cross-border trade and a more favourable position in global value chains (Figure 1.4), thus becoming more sustainable.

1.5 SUMMARY

Our framework recasts the BRI from a new integrated perspective highlighting the essential regional nature of economic corridors. Given their length, these corridors carry the BRI's impacts on globalisation, urbanisation and development across long distances, capable of touching and changing a vast swath of urban and rural places in less and least developed countries. Along and through the corridors, the BRI's varied impacts are channelled by the mechanisms of connectivity, infrastructure and sustainability. Our framework conceptualises the BRI as an unprecedented set of corridor-centric regionalisations that influence globalisation, urbanisation and development from a variety of middle scales and positions. This corridor regionalisation creates multiple layers of encounters between global, national and local scales and actors in the BRI. This framework (Figure 1.5) guides a three-pronged analysis of a trio of cases leading to policy recommendations at the end of chapters 2–4.

https://doi.org/10.1080/2578711X.2020.1823710

2. THE BRI AND GLOBALISATION

2.1 INTRODUCTION

We argue that the BRI can be a synergistic force in recent history to reshape the course of globalisation, especially the regional dimension and consequences of globalisation. This potential epochal transformation has two parallel and linked processes. On one track, the BRI challenges the ideology, drivers, sequence and outcomes of globalisation in the contemporary era led by the West, especially its large multinational corporations over the past decades. On the other, the BRI favours a more targeted development of economic cooperation in trade and investment between China and the Global South, prioritising partnerships with less and least developed countries. The BRI's double-sided interaction with both Western advanced and developing economies has emerged from the context of important shifts in globalisation vis-à-vis China's shifted global position and magnified importance. In this chapter we first present evidence on shifts in both globalisation and China's position. We then compare the stages of the positions and roles of the West versus China in globalisation. To demonstrate China's new leading role in globalisation via creating large-scale trade and transport connections, we conduct a case study of the China–Europe Freight Train (CEFT).

2.2 SHIFTING GLOBALISATION AND CHINA'S IMPORTANCE

Globalisation, in a primarily economic sense, can be defined as increasing financial flow and commodity trade across national borders, augmented by progress in technologies of transportation and communications. The shift of economic globalisation, especially since the financial crisis of 2008, appears to have run into the BRI's arrival and progression since 2013. This partial connection or meeting between two strong forces, at least temporally, reflects an earlier and deeper convergence between shifting globalisation and the changed position of China in the global economy before the BRI.

First, global trade has lost steam as the share of output moving across the world's borders fell from 28.1% in 2007 to 22.5% (US$17.3 trillion) in 2017.[1] While not a fully comparable indicator, China has accounted for an increasingly larger share of the world's trade in goods reaching 11.4% in 2017. Second, global trade in services had grown more than 60% faster than goods trade and reached US$5.1 trillion in 2017. If counting 'free' digital data flows (estimated to be US$8.3 trillion annually), trade in services is already more valuable than trade in goods.[2] China, however, accounted for only about 6.4% of global services trade in 2017. Third, with a declined comparative advantage in cheap labour, over 80% of today's global goods trade is not from a low- to a high-wage country. The share of lower labour cost in labour-intensive manufacturing dropped from 55% in 2005 to 43% in 2017.[3] China's continued dependence

---

[1] McKinsey (2019) *Globalization in Transition: The Future of Trade and Value Chains*. New York: McKinsey Global Institute.
[2] McKinsey (2019), see Reference 1.
[3] McKinsey (2019); see Reference 1.

https://doi.org/10.1080/2578711X.2020.1823711

on labour-intensive manufacturing has become a competitive disadvantage, with growing pressure on moving up the production chain or ladder.

China's accelerated industrial upgrading has added a new dimension to its global power and influence. One illustration is that if we use value added to measure trade and economic relationships, China's trade deficit with the United States around 2015 would have been about US$200 billion instead of almost US$400 billion.[4] This means China had been selling to and buying from the United States in higher value-added parts. In a similar vein, China has accelerated its investment in technology and innovation by spending US$293 billion in 2018 as the world's second largest research and development (R&D) investor.[5] China's share of the world's total patents rose almost six-fold between 2000 and 2014, only slightly behind the United States (Box 2.1).[6]

> **Box 2.1   Shares of the world's total patents:** 2000: China (5%) and United States (32%); and 2014: China (28%) and United States (29%)

As a global innovation leader that sustains some traditional manufacturing, China has stretched its occupied space and sphere of influence across the global economic hierarchy. By one indicator, 20% of global trade in manufacturing intermediates originates in China.[7] Vietnam, for example, depended on China for 52% of network products in electronic communication in 2018, up from 34% in 2000.[8] If we take into account China's largest contribution to global economic growth averaging 28.1% annually during 2013–18,[9] it is easy to see the considerable global impact of the Chinese economy disrupted by the COVID-19 pandemic in early 2020. Of the approximately US$50 billion in exports lost along global value chains, China is the central source of negative impact on a variety of industries, such as machinery, automotive and chemicals for the European Union (EU), machinery and precision instruments for the United States, and communication equipment for Vietnam. Several countries stood to lose greatly from the estimated US$1 trillion loss from the global economy dominated by China's exports (Box 2.2).[10] While global foreign direct investment (FDI) declined by 23% from US$1.87 trillion in 2016 to US$1.5 trillion in 2017, and fell again by

[4] Donnan D and Leatherby L (2019) *Globalization Isn't Dying, It's Just Evolving*. Bloomberg, 23 July. Available at: www.bloomberg.com/graphics/2019-globalization/.

[5] McKinsey (2019) *China and the World: Inside the Dynamics of a Changing Relationship*. New York: McKinsey Global Institute.

[6] McKinsey (2019); see Reference 1.

[7] United Nations Conference on Trade and Development (UNCTAD) (2020) *Global Trade Impact of the Coronavirus (COVID-19) Epidemic*. Technical Note prepared by the Division on International Trade and Commodities, 4 March.

[8] Majumder S (2020) Coronavirus hits global value chain: second thoughts on 'assemble in India'. *Eurasia Review*, 14 March. Available at: www.eurasiareview.com/14032020-coronavirus-hits-global-value-chain-second-thoughts-on-assemble-in-india-analysis/?utm_source=feedburner&utm_medium=email&utm_campaign=Feed%3A+eurasiareview%2FVsnE+%28Eurasia+Review%29.

[9] Xinhua (2019) *China Rises to Top Engine of Global Economic Growth in 70 Years*. Xinhua, 29 August. Available at: www.xinhuanet.com/english/2019-08/29/c_138348922.htm.

[10] UNCTAD (2020); see Reference 7.

13% to US$1.3 trillion in 2018,[11] China's investment in multiple billions so far rising to trillions through the BRI over time helps offset the shrinking pool and pace of global investment.

From a normal or abnormal (crisis) global perspective, China is a central influencer. Given the range of impacted economies and sectors due to COVID-19, China matters a great deal to the BRI partners within and across regional boundaries. China's impact on the BRI countries, as discussed in the introduction, is shaped by how its domestic regional economies have latched onto the six transborder corridors. Chinese corporate actors as central players in the BRI in turn forge this inside-out regional connectivity.

> **Box 2.2 From the disruption by the China-dominated exports in the global economy:**
>
> - The European Union could lose US$15.6 billion
> - The United States US$5.8 billion
> - Japan US$5.2 billion
> - Korea US$3.8 billion
> - Taiwan US$2.6 billion
> - Vietnam US$2.3 billion

With 110 Global Fortune 500 companies, comparable with the United States, China can leverage this large corporate asset and power to support the BRI. However, these top ranked Chinese companies are anchored in the domestic market, with only 18% of their revenues earned overseas versus 44% for S&P 500 firms.[12] Yet China's large companies are much more globally oriented in the construction industry, which dominates the BRI's prevalent activity in infrastructure provision. According to the *Engineering News-Record*, seven of the top 10 largest global contractors, ranked according to construction revenue generated outside of each company's home country, were Chinese companies, which also accounted for 30 of the top 100 global contractors, the most of any nation.[13] This global strength in construction coupled with China's sustained manufacturing prowess necessitates a comparative rethink on historical, contemporary and future globalisation.

2.3 THE WEST- VERSUS CHINA-LED GLOBALISATIONS

Globalisation is an inherently uneven spatial process that tracks the unequal cross-national distribution of economic and political power. This power is leveraged by certain dominant nations' comparative and competitive strengths during a given era of world history. From a historical but not ancient perspective, the rise of the West to world dominance through the Industrial Revolution, subsequent colonisation and post-war dominance has accelerated globalisation. This West-led globalisation, however, has taken a step back since the global financial crisis and a further step back since the election of Donald Trump and the rhetoric of 'America First' and withdrawal from the Trans-Pacific

---

[11] United Nations (2018) *World Investment Report 2018*. New York: United Nations; United Nations (2019) *World Investment Report 2019*. New York: United Nations.

[12] McKinsey (2019); see Reference 5.

[13] *Engineering News-Record* (ENR) (2018) Top 250 global contractors 1–100. *Engineering News-Record* (ENR). August. Available at: www.enr.com/toplists/2018-Top-250-Global-Contractors-1.

Partnership. While Brexit may not be exactly anti-global, it reflects a backlash against such practices of globalisation as open borders and immigration. COVID-19 set the era of West-led globalisation back a big notch as the United States and Europe suffered greater health and economic losses than China. Against the West's recent retreats from globalisation, China has stepped up to the front and centre of the pro-globalisation plate. President Xi Jinping spoke confidently about the virtue of open trade and the danger in retreating from it at the 2017 World Economic Forum. China further asserted itself on a besieged world stage through its earlier and more successful control of COVID-19 and providing medical and healthcare assistance to many countries, including the hard-hit Western European countries. This series of turns begs a comparative look at globalisation led by the West versus an emerging China-led globalisation (Table 2.1).

Table 2.1 The West- versus China-led globalisations:

Period: Stage:	16th century → stage 1	1750s → stage 2	1970s → stage 3	1980s → stage 4
West-led globalisation	Ocean exploration/colonialism/imperalism	Trade/manufacturing	Growing and dominant services	New knowledge economy/information and communication technology (ICT)
	(European expansion and quest for natural resources)	(International division of labour with unequal exchange and development)	(Low-end such as fast food and high value-added such as finance; home–abroad)	(Value chain integration, service trade, digitech, fintech and artificial intelligence (AI))

Period: Stage:	Old Silk Road (~CE) → stage 1	1980s → stage 2	2000s → stage 3	New Silk Road 2010s → stage 4
China-led globalisation	Regional and long-distance trade	Manufacturing/exports	Infrastructure provision	Integrated (BRI as a key driver)
	(Segmented and connected trade routes from western China to Central Asia and Europe)	(Starting with low-end assembly and later upgrading to medium- and high-end production)	(Overseas urban construction and connections) services (catching up from a low level, rising consumption)	(Innovations in manufacturing, construction, high-tech services, and digital and e-commerce platforms)

Source: Lead author.

Table 2.1 charts a pair of schematic trajectories of the period, stage and main driver of the West-led globalisation versus China-led new globalisation. Taking a long historical perspective, we see China as a much earlier leader in globalisation dating from the ancient Silk Road around the beginning of the common era as the earliest stage of globalisation. This continued for a full millennium to around 1000 when the city of Quanzhou, half way between Shanghai and Hong Kong on China's coast, two much later global cities,

https://doi.org/10.1080/2578711X.2020.1823711

prospered as a dominant global market, drawing goods and traders from Java, India and Africa.[14] The West began to lead on globalisation after the 1500s and China's inward turn following the last international initiative of General Zheng He in the Ming dynasty (who led a maritime expedition to East Africa in the first half of the 1400s). Despite these periodic maritime contacts on and from its eastern seaboard, China remained largely a continental land power that maintained a mostly western orientation from the early days of the ancient Silk Road. Ironically, the West (Portugal and Spain) took a page from General Zheng in exploring and then exploiting the world through its expeditions on the high seas, starting in 1492. While this period constituted one of several ages of globalisation,[15] we see it as the beginning of West-led globalisation.

The West's role in leading globalisation became stronger during the 1700s when the Industrial Revolution brought about a second stage of globalisation. It fuelled the West's long-run dominance in trade, manufacturing and international division of labour well into the 20th century (Table 2.1). As Western economies began to deindustrialise in the early 1970s, they exported advanced services such as finance, ushering in a third stage of contemporary globalisation. While continuing, this stage has progressed into a fourth and current stage since the 1980s. Featuring the knowledge economy and the tech sector as the leading edge, this new West-led globalisation has bridged and blended the critical elements of globalisation over the preceding two stages in creating innovative industries such as fintech. This globalisation has produced or worsened inequalities with a relatively small number of winners and many losers in the West and beyond. It leads such scholars as Dani Rodrik to contend that economic globalisation cannot coexist with both democratic politics and national sovereignty, one of which must be sacrificed when pursuing globalisation.[16] This internal dilemma has prompted and become more prominent in the recent wave of West (primarily US)-led deglobalisation.

Fast forward China-led globalisation from the Silk Road era to the contemporary age and we see China re-emerge as a latecomer compared with the West. Geographically, China leads a new round of globalisation more by making new land-based connections from its vast inland toward the west, while the West launched its initial globalisation through colonial expansion from its much smaller and fragmented territories in Europe on the sea. Like the West economically, China rose as a leader of globalisation from its powerful manufacturing base. Unlike the West for a long time, China only began to dominate global manufacturing after receiving massive investment from the West that translated into rapid industrialisation from the early 1980s. Even more different from the West and against an underdeveloped service sector, China turned to infrastructure construction as another domain where it could lead the world from around 2000, with the second turn to its western region (Table 1.1).

[14] Hansen V (2020) *The Year 1000: When Explorers Connected the World – And Globalization Began*. New York: Scribner.

[15] Sachs J (2020) *The Ages of Globalization: Geography, Technology, and Institutions*. New York: Columbia University Press.

[16] Rodrik D (2011) *The Globalization Paradox: Democracy and the Future of the World Economy*. New York: W. W. Norton.

https://doi.org/10.1080/2578711X.2020.1823711

Similar to its wide and deep manufacturing foundation, China has built the world's longest highways and largest high-speed train network in the shortest time as the anchoring parts of a massive new infrastructure system. With this vast accumulated experience, expertise and capacity, China has been building out into many parts of the world and thus earned its leadership spot in infrastructure globalisation that defines a third stage. This dominant role in domestic and global infrastructure provision coupled with continued upgrading in its manufacturing prowess and growing strength in technological innovation has placed China into leading a new stage of integrated globalisation, with the BRI as its primary driver. China's rise to global economic leadership benefited from growing connection and integration with the West through trade and industrial division of labour during their respective second stages of globalisation.

With its superiority in global infrastructure construction and its more balanced approach to globalisation, China has diverged from the West during the two recent stages and thus begun to lead a different globalisation through the BRI. In contrast to the West's super-mobility of financial capital across space, China's infrastructure production in and across far-flung, disparate places creates immobile fixations that can either facilitate or forestall a more productive and beneficial spatial reconfiguration of capital–labour relations.[17] Leading a different globalisation does not mean that China will lead the only globalisation. It makes more sense to view the BRI as giving China a great opportunity to introduce new elements and practices that may reshape the current globalisation into a more inclusive and equitable one to the greater benefit of poorer countries and peoples. This is likely to instigate a strong scenario for the coexistence and competition between both the West and China-led globalisations as the BRI gains more traction and reaction going forward.

A litmus test on if China can successfully lead a new globalisation concerns its ability to pursue and achieve a more inclusive globalisation through the BRI.[18] It means China needs to do much better with less and least developed countries that have not advanced under West-led globalisation. To illuminate this test, we turn to Paul Collier's *The Bottom Billion* (2007),[19] the peak point of West-led globalisation before the financial crisis in 2008 that set it back a big step through protectionism and populism. Collier saw a divergence in the developing world. Several countries, including China and India with a huge combined population, had benefited from globalisation and moved into the global middle class while 1 billion poor people spread among 58 countries had been trapped in poverty at the bottom of the development ladder. Besides the four traps for the bottom 1 billion (see the left column of Appendix A), Collier attributed this bifurcated shift to much of Western investment and international development assistance flowing into the larger and rapidly developing countries at the expense of the bottom 1 billion.

[17] Chen X, Fu N, Zhou S and Xu G (2020) The spatial decoupling and recombination of capital and labour: Understanding the new dynamics and flows between China and Southeast Asia. In P S Aulakh and P Kelly (eds.), *Asian Connections: Linking Mobilities of Labour and Capital*, pp. 120–150. Delhi: Cambridge University Press.

[18] Liu W and Dunford M (2016) Inclusive globalization: Unpacking China's Belt and Road Initiative. *Area Development and Policy*, 1(3): 323–340.

[19] Collier P (2007) *The Bottom Billion: Why the Poorest Countries are Failing and What Can Be Done About It*. Oxford: Oxford University Press.

While facing west and leading to Europe primarily, the six BRI regional corridors pass through mostly developing countries in much of Asia, the Middle East and East Africa, as well as the less developed East–Central European economies. This turns our attention to the connection between the BRI as China-led globalisation and as an ambitious China-led effort to jump start a new round of South–South cooperation. As the bottom a billion has benefited little from Western aid and investment, the BRI favours the less and least developing countries as targets for Chinese aid and investment. To lend some credence to this, we have matched the BRI countries and those with BRI cooperation agreements with the World Bank's four categories of countries based on their per capita incomes (see Appendix A).

More countries in the two lowest-income categories were either full participants in the BRI or signed more cooperation agreements (87.3% and 77.5%) than in the other two categories (Box 2.3). The low middle-income category has the largest percentages of countries as BRI partners or with cooperation agreements. Several countries, including Cambodia, Laos, Myanmar and Pakistan, in this category belonged to the bottom 1 billion about 15 years ago, but have been most com-mitted to the BRI since 2013. While the BRI is heavily oriented to less and least developing countries, it has drawn 69.9% and 42.6% of participation and coop-eration from countries in the upper middle- and high-income countries (Box 2.3), pointing to a global scope

> **Box 2.3   Percentages of BRI countries or countries with BRI agreements in four income categories:**
>
> - High income: 23.8% and 18.8% (total = 42.6%)
> - Upper middle income: 38.3% and 31.6% (69.9%)
> - Low middle income: 42.6% and 44.7% (87.3%)
> - Low income: 19.4% and 58.1% (77.5%)
>
> *Source*: See Appendix A

of a receptive interest and willing participation in the BRI. Moreover, the BRI has involved a set of Western advanced economies in the high-income category such as Germany and the UK that have cooperation with the BRI.

The involvement of Western European countries renders the China–Europe Freight Train (CEFT) the first case study for examining how the BRI corridors have exerted a global impact from their transregional con-nections spanning countries in different income categories. It offers a fresh case for demonstrating the BRI's impact on globalisation through the CEFT.

2.4   REGIONAL CORRIDORS' CONNECTIVE GLOBAL IMPACT: THE CHINA–EUROPE FREIGHT TRAIN (CEFT)

Through our analytical framework in Figure 1.5, we examine the BRI's role in reshaping globalisation through the connectivity lens. Figure 2.1 reveals a rough geographical affinity and overlap between three BRI corridors (numbers 1–3 in Figure 1.1) (see also Box 1.1) and three CEFT trunk routes (Easter, Western

Figure 2.1   The China–Europe freight train's trunk routes

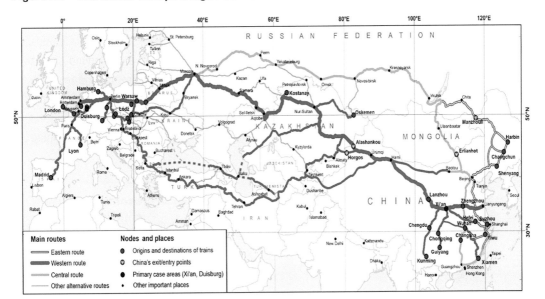

Source: Modified from Chen X (2020), fig. 3.

and Central). We focus on the Western route primarily to clarify the global impact of these long-range logistics connections (Figure 2.1).

2.4.1   Connections and growth

Since the first CEFT (Chongqing–Duisburg) line was rolled out in 2011, the number of CEFT routes has grown to 65 that connect around 60 cities in China to over 50 international cities including 44 cities in 15 European countries and the remaining ones in 14 (mostly Central) Asian countries.[20] The Western route mainly runs along but extends the new Eurasian Land Bridge all the way into the heart of Europe, and carries around 80% of all CEFT trains.[21] It also spins off alternative lines that branch south to lap with the BRI's China–Central Asia–West Asia Corridor and countries that are less developed. The Western route of the CEFT includes the world's longest cargo train running 13,000 km across eight countries between the Chinese city of Yiwu near the coast and Madrid, while another route connects Yiwu directly to London.

As a new global connector, the CEFT is anchored to several large Chinese cities, mostly located in central and western China, as points or stations of departure and return destinations. Of the 16 major CEFT cities

---

[20] By 2018, the CEFT had been officially designated and known as the China Railways Express (CRE). We prefer the acronym CEFT to convey the bidirectional and two-ended nature and form of this transcontinental rail freight network.

[21] Bucsky P (2020) The Iron Silk Road: How important is it? *Area Development and Policy*, 5(2): 146–166.

in China, nine are intermodal hubs and the other seven have the added production bases (Figure 2.2). This spatial expression of the CEFT is logically consistent with the intended goal and process of China's second turn, that is, accelerating the development of major interior cities and enhancing their roles in stimulating the less developed inland region. As expected, almost all the important cities in central China (Changsha, Wuhan and Zhengzhou) and western China (Chengdu, Urumqi and Xi'an) are prominent players in the CEFT. The participation of other important cities (Hangzhou, Suzhou and Yiwu) in coastal provinces, including the premier coastal metropolis of Shanghai, points to a wider networked geography of connections between land-based logistics in the interior and export-oriented industrial centres near major seaports. Figure 2.2 also displays four small border cities of China serving as exit/entry points for CEFTs.

Figure 2.2   The China–Europe freight train and China's regional realignment

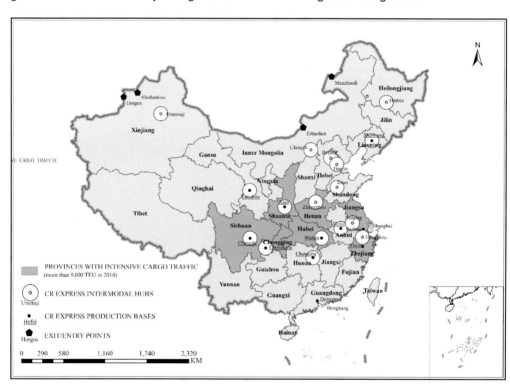

Source: Same as for Figure 2.1.

The CEFT's connectivity over long distances and vast geographies aside, it has grown rapidly over a few short years. While there were only 17 trips in 2011, the number of trips soared to 6363 in 2018, which almost equalled the total number of trips in the previous seven years. By March 2019, the CEFT made over 14,000 round-trips. The total number of trips in 2019 exceeded the 2018 peak with the figure for the first seven months of 2020 pushing the annual total to surpass 2019 (Figure 2.3), for reasons mentioned below. In 2018, the total goods volume of the CEFT trips reached US$16 billion, dwarfing the US$600 million in

Figure 2.3   Growth of the China–Europe freight train, 2011–20

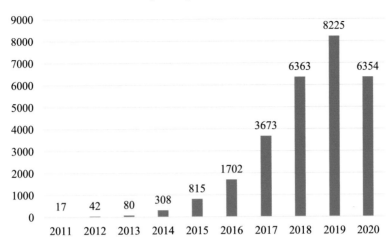

Sources: Graphed China Railway data first reported in *The South China Morning Post*, 20 August 2019; data from China State Railway Group Co. Available online at: https://mp.weixin.qq.com/s/NeFH0kLHP_Ak01dSONoNvA [Accessed 3 July 2020]; and data for 2020 pertain to the January–July period. Available online at: https://mp.weixin.qq.com/s/RV4yDYChkUc5hLNAR010ng and https://news.cgtn.com/news/2020-08-09/China-Europe-freight-trains-up-68-in-July-SOBKSUtlMQ/index.html

2011.[22] Despite this rapid growth, the CEFT's unbalanced network structure has limited its more symmetrical development. Before 2014, every trip headed in one direction: from China to Europe. However, the return trips began to grow in 2016 and accounted roughly for one-third of the combined trips. Of all 3673 trips in 2017, 1225 (33.4%) trains went from Europe to China.[23] In 2018, the share of Europe-to-China trains rose to 42.0% of all trips. This evidence indicates an end of the 'one-way street' with all trains going from China to Europe during the CEFT's first decade.

2.4.2   Xi'an's resurgence as a hub

The CEFT's rapid growth over a relatively short time span has a lot to with China's cities serving as powerful hubs that have initiated and sustained more train routes to more European cities. This local-to-global reach originates from and is augmented by the strong municipal government in interior China. The ancient city of Xi'an is a compelling example. The city has invoked the metaphor of the 'Iron Silk Road' as if the freight trains in the 21st century were the camels of 2000 years ago. Xi'an has named its CEFT lines after the old city name of 'Chang'an' (Forever Peace), which was used for the ancient capital of several Chinese dynasties until it was renamed Xi'an (Western Peace) in 1369. Drawing from this historical image and identity for the

---

[22]CGTN (2019) *Data Tells: How China's Train Routes are Boosting Trade and Making It Cheaper.* CGTN.com, 19 April. Available at: https://news.cgtn.com/news/3d3d674d3351444d34457a6333566d54/index.html.

[23]Jakóbowski J, Popławski K and Kaczmarski M (2018) *The Silk Railroad: The EU–China Rail Connections: Background, Actors, Interests.* Warsaw: Centre for Eastern Studies.

present opportunity to forge new logistical ties to the West, the Xi'an municipal government has provided direct financing and indirect operation to the International Trade and Logistics Park (ITLP), which sends and receives CEFTs. It awarded the status of a new development zone to the Bureau of Port Activities, which has in turn created the ITLP as a state-owned enterprise (SOE). In this organisational set-up, the municipal government is the de facto operator of the ITLP and thus aims to keep the CEFT at the front and centre of Xi'an's development.

The state bent on building Xi'an as a logistics hub has attracted lead logistics firms as partners. One of the world's top international logistics firms, Nippon Express established a branch in Xi'an's Comprehensive Bonded Zone in August 2013. In December 2018, Nippon Express sent its first freight train from the ITLP to Duisburg, Germany. The train carried 41 containers filled with high-resolution liquid-crystal display panels, high-end printers and cameras, air compressors and other high-valued-added products, with the entire cargo valued at US$17 million and setting the single-train record in freight value for 2018. Running trains from the ITLP to Europe, Nippon Express helps Japanese companies with factories in China ship parts, equipment and finished products brought by air and sea from Japan directly to Germany. In November 2019, DHL Global Forwarding and Xi'an International Inland Port Investment & Development Group Co. Ltd launched the fastest rail service from Xi'an to Hamburg and Neuss, an important logistics hub on the Rhine River, cutting the transit time from 17 to 10–12 days.[24]

To expand global production and trade connections to Europe, Xi'an has also attracted manufacturing companies in both assembly and supply that (re)locate there in order to ship both finished products and parts to European markets more quickly than ocean shipping and cost-effectively than air. Having moved (back) from Shenzhen to Xi'an, electronics firm A, which had originated locally and exports to Hungary, now saves a lot of transport time by rail versus by sea, from 45 to 15 days. This allows the firm to reduce the cycle of its order placement and supply chain coordination from 90 to 30–45 days and thus be better able to react to price changes and other potential risks.

As another example, Volvo has benefited greatly from running a new regular train between Xi'an and Ghent, Belgium. In June 2018, a CEFT train departed from Ghent and arrived at Xi'an vehicle port with 160 European-made Volvo XC90 SUVs and V40 hatchbacks, after 16 days and more than 10,000 km. One year later, a CEFT loaded with 160 XC60 SUVs arrived in Ghent from Xi'an. Made at Volvo's plant in the city of Chengdu, the XC60s would be sold in 25 European countries, including Italy and Germany.[25] With faster customs e-clearance at Xi'an's designated vehicle port, wealthy buyers of imported Volvos in interior China

[24] *Indonesia Shipping Gazette* (2019) DHL and Xi'an Group launch fastest rail freight service between China and Germany, 5 November. Available at: https://indoshippinggazette.com/2019/dhl-and-xi'an-group-launches-fastest-rail-freight-service-between-china-and-germany/.

[25] *China Daily* (2018) New China Railway express train service imports Volvo Cars to Xi'an. *China Daily*, 15 June. Available online at: www.chinadaily.com.cn/a/201806/15/WS5b2387b9a310010f8f59d39f.html; *China Daily* (2019) Volvo's China-made SUVs exported to European market. *China Daily*, 8 July. Available at: www.chinadaily.com.cn/a/201907/08/WS5d22d625a3105895c2e7c40f.html.

https://doi.org/10.1080/2578711X.2020.1823711

can receive their delivered cars in one-third of the time as ocean transport to the eastern ports such as Shanghai followed by westward overland transport.

Both examples above reflect the increasing introduction of digital technology such as China's Beidou Navigation Satellite System-enabled tracking and wireless smart coding on containers for cross-border customs clearance that have enhanced speed and accuracy in train travel over long distances and across international boundaries and on-time arrival and transfer to spur lines and extended destinations in Europe (see below). This merges the loosely coordinated Digital Silk Road (DSR) initiative with the BRI's CEFT in creating a synergistic effect on the reach and efficiency of new global logistical connectivity. It is capable of improving the CEFT as an 'Iron Silk Road' through some facilitating elements of the DSR.

From just one exemplary city of Xi'an along only the Western route, the CEFT has spun new trade and production connections from China to advanced Western European and transitional East–Central economies and a large number of their cities, through a few hubs such as Kaliningrad in Russia, Duisburg in Germany and Małaszewicze in Poland (Figure 2.4). While these countries belong to the upper and upper middle-income categories (see Appendix A), the London–Yiwu and Xi'an–Duisburg train routes have created unexpected economic and logistics ties between cities with large laps in stature and influence in the global urban hierarchy. Via the new direct freight train connection to London, Yiwu – the world's largest sourcing centre for small merchandise – now serves a more global, albert specialised, nodal function. This level and scale of new global connectivity would not have emerged without the length and shape of the BRI corridors that have spurred the CEFT.

Figure 2.4   Xi'an's growing freight routes to Europe and South and West Asia

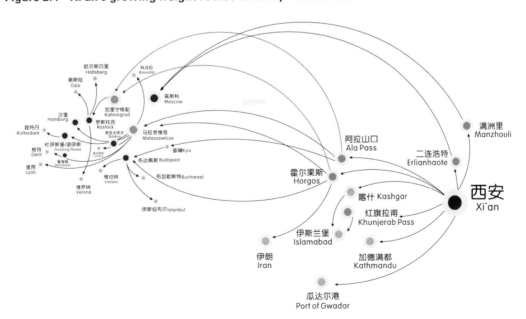

Source: Xi'an ITLP WeChat public platform, with permission

In 2020, Xi'an launched new freight services to Istanbul in Turkey, Islamabad in Pakistan and Kathmandu in Nepal via challenging multimodal transport connections through remote and difficult terrains (Figure 2.4). The Istanbul-bound train went through Central Asia and crossed the Caspian Sea to reach Baku Port from where unloaded containers would be delivered to Turkey by the Baku–Tbilisi–Kars Railway. The train to Islamabad would run to Kashgar across Xinjiang and then trucked to the destination in northern Pakistan through the Khunjerab Pass, 5000 masl on the China–Pakistan border. To reach Kathmandu, the train from Xi'an ploughed along the Qinghai–Tibet Railway, which also reaches 5000 masl, to Lhasa. From there the cargo would be trucked or carried on an extended rail line to Shigatse, Tibet's second largest city, from where it would be trucked to the Nepalese capital through the Tibetan border town and land port of Gyirong over the Himalayas. Following a feasibility study for a new cross-border railway from Shigatse to Kathmandu via Gyirong in October 2019, China and Nepal launched the field survey for building the segment of the rail from Shigatse to Gyirong in March 2020. Compared with the traditional sea–land routes from China to South Asia, these overland train–truck routes, or the Xi'an–Kathmandu trail route in the future, are faster and more direct. The latter will also give western China a more convenient and efficient physical entry into South Asia's trading network where the Xi'an–Islamabad train–truck route can connect directly to the CPEC, another of the six BRI corridors (number 6 in Figure 1.1), from northern Pakistan to the Port of Gwadar on the Arabian Sea.

Back to the cross-border train routes already in operation, the CEFT has even sustained existing and created new China–Europe trade and logistics ties through the disruptive economic impact of COVID-19. During the first three months of 2020 when China was dealing with the COVID-19 pandemic and struggling to reopen the economy, 27 trains from Xi'an carried 3377 XC60s to the European markets through a fast and secure system from truck to train without exposing the new cars to potential virus contamination.[26] In April 2020, Xi'an sent the very first block train to Tilburg, the Netherlands, carrying dedicated photovoltaic products made by Longi Green Energy Co., based in Shaanxi province. During the first quarter of 2020, 649 westbound trains left Xi'an for around 40 countries in Europe and Central Asia, up 2.4 times over the same period of 2019, which contributed to the CEFT's overall growth at the national level (Figure 2.4). The cargo's range was widened to about 5000 specific products in autos, kitchenware, daily necessities and nine other categories.[27]

As COVID-19 disrupted international mail cargo by reducing Europe-bound flights from Shanghai in spring 2020, a lot of this cargo, including urgently needed medical supplies, was quickly trucked to the city of Yiwu from where the redirected cargo was carried to Europe by freight trains. On 31 May, the 200th CEFT (Yiwu) train for 2020 left Yiwu for Madrid. Through 31 May, this route carried 16,672 containers, up 72%

[26] Jiangxi TV Station (2020) The China–Europe freight train for Volvo returns to normal. Jiangxi TV Station, 8 April. Available at: https://cn.chinadaily.com.cn/a/202004/08/WS5e8d742ba310395ca8f746bb.html.
[27] *The China–Europe Freight Train Newsletter* (2020) The China–Europe freight train (the Chang'an) – The first Xi'an–Netherlands photovoltaic block train launched. *The China–Europe Freight Train Newsletter*, 2 May. Available at: https://mp.weixin.qq.com/s/xxEMnS5p1swBcSD1yd7sEw.

https://doi.org/10.1080/2578711X.2020.1823711

from the first five months of 2019.[28] During the global pandemic, DB Schenker, a division of German rail operator Deutsche Bahn AG, worked with Xi'an-based CEFT in sending 10 containers with medical protective equipment to virus-stricken Italy in May 2020.

While the CEFT's growth through the pandemic shows its resilience, it has been sustained since the outset by government subsidies that vary between US$2000 and US$4000 per container, equalling almost half or more of the actual per container cost, or between 40% and 50% of the cost for 2017. The very aggressive Xi'an government even pushed the subsidy up to cover 100% of the shipping cost.[29] This puts strong pressure on generating more market demand for the CEFT inside China, a main challenge to its second turn to western China and the BRI. With the local and provincial subsidies scheduled to expire by 2022 and to re-energise the BRI through the pandemic, the national government in July 2020 decided to allocate around US$70 million form the central budget to support the consolidation of five major CEFT hubs including Xi'an. Considering that a fewer hubs would be more efficient,[30] this new national government measure should make the next phase of CEFT development more efficient and sustainable. It reaffirms the BRI as the driving force behind the CEFT that has created strong and resilient logistics connections between China and a large and diverse number of international regions and cities west of China's western land border.

2.5   SUMMARY AND POLICY RECOMMENDATIONS

China has emerged as a new or alternative leader of globalisation. Dating to its ancient origin in the Silk Road, this powerful role stems from China's fast economic growth and global rise relative to the West. As the world's second largest economy with shifting competitive advantages in dominant manufacturing and disadvantages in rising labour costs, China has led and driven a different mix of globalising activities (Figure 2.1) through the BRI's regional corridors. This has spun cross-border connections with important regional and local outcomes. Using the CEFT as an in-depth case study, we have shown that the growing flow of freight cargo through Eurasia has emerged as a new regional pathway for more global trade along the ancient Silk Road trading routes.

To draw policy lessons from the BRI's impact on globalisation, we reiterate and update a few practical aspects of the CEFT's global connective reach. First, the CEFT relies on several major cities in interior China as multiple sources of freight cargo. These cities also attract and redirect a greater volume of cargo flow from the large and productive centres in China's coastal region to Europe. Second, the CEFT has benefited from the increasing weight of logistics and supply chains in the global economy. It has become a

---

[28] *Yicai* (2020); Change in the CEFT: a number of nodal stations for the future, 6 June. Available at: www.yicai.com/news/100655204.html.

[29] Tjia X N L (2020) The unintended consequences of politicization of the Belt and Road's China–Europe freight train initiative. *China Journal*, 83: 58–78.

[30] Bucsky (2020); see Reference 21.

'geologistics' strategy for China[31] to reignite sluggish exports through land-based trade routes with Europe and Central Asia. Third, by adding more train lines to more cities and countries in Europe, Central Asia, West Asia and South Asia more recently, the CEFT has extended a large network of freight rail connections across several geographically contiguous and adjacent regions. This calls for policy responses from all the engaged players and stakeholder to sustain the CEFT-driven global trade for greater connected benefits (Box 2.4).

Box 2.4   Policy recommendations for the BRI versus globalisation regarding CEFT:

- At the most general level, we recommend policy responses from the international community to the global impact of the BRI to be based on a clear understanding of its drivers from deep inside China and its domestic economic transformation. This helps avoid the kind of international and national policies that react and counter the BRI's as China's grand geopolitical strategy for global hegemony
- At the cross-regional and sector levels, we advocate policies from any quarters to react to the CEFT as a new regional corridor of logistical connections among a large number of countries. This will encourage countries working with the CEFT to expand their trade, especially exports to China. The EU can grow and enlarge its share of China trade from a mere 2% carried by overland freight train, while Central Asia can continue to diverse its trade with China by exporting its rich agricultural products to China beyond just oil, gas and minerals
- At the transborder and translocal levels, we encourage policies to create direct cooperation between cities across the international boundaries along the CEFT routes. This can expand the inter-city links already in place to spin off more spur lines to draw in unconnected marginal places into the overall network
- At the firm level, we propose policies that incentivise more logistics and manufacturing companies such as DHL, Nippon Express and Volvo from multiple countries to work closely with subnational governments in generating more freight CEFT cargo from manufacturers with supply chains along and at either end of and along the train routes
- Assuming that these policies complement one another, they can add up to a broader synergistic role in sustaining the CEFT as a large-scale and resilient logistics network as proven during the global pandemic. These policies are needed to support the young CEFT to grow and mature into a truly global logistics network that enables the more traditional mode of freight train to supplement and complement maritime containerised shipping and air cargo, especially at times such as when a pandemic severely disrupts global supply chains

---

[31] Rimmer P (2020) *China's Global Vision and Actions: Reactions to Belt, Road and Beyond.* Cheltenham: Edward Elgar.

  https://doi.org/10.1080/2578711X.2020.1823711

3. THE BRI AND URBANISATION

3.1 INTRODUCTION

The BRI's impact on globalisation is entangled with a set of strong and significant ties between the BRI and urbanisation. The BRI's connections to global urbanisation also originate from inside China and its first geographical turn to the coast (Table 1.1). The establishment of Shenzhen as a special economic zone (SEZ) in 1979 constituted the local origin of China's rapid urbanisation that has since transformed a primarily agricultural landscape and economy and begun to affect urban development beyond China. As the defining feature of China's urbanisation, infrastructure construction is key to our framing for and analysis of how the BRI has produced powerful an inside-out impact on global and regional urbanisation beyond China.

This chapter begins with a historical perspective on the infrastructure state for pulling contemporary insights into the reach and power of the Chinese infrastructure state embodied by the BRI. We then examine infrastructure construction as the key to understanding China's own urbanisation as the extended source of its external impact on global urbanisation. We illustrate the coupling of both arguments through a paired or paralleled case study of the Laotian border town of Borten as a China-built new city and the China–Laos Railway (CLR) as a cross-border transport infrastructure project.

3.2 THE BRI'S INFRASTRUCTURE REACH AND POWER

Urbanisation and infrastructure are intertwined and reciprocal in how they depend on and influence each other. From a long historical perspective, infrastructure tended to lag the pace and scale of urbanisation. When trading outposts along the ancient Silk Road emerged as early urban settlements, they had minimum lodging facilities for long-distance traders and were linked by slow caravans moving on dirt and muddy tracks. As cities and towns in Western Europe grew in scale and influence through industrialisation in the 18th century, there was a severe shortage of adequate housing for factory workers and inadequate municipal infrastructure for pleasant urban life. Fast forward to late 20th-century China, rapid and large-scale infrastructure build-up became part and parcel of the speeding and scaling of urbanisation. Furthermore, infrastructure often outpaced urbanisation as newly built 'ghost cities' sitting empty of people and activity. While some of this idle infrastructure has since been partially or fully used due to catch-up demand from continued urbanisation, infrastructure-led urbanisation in China and extending from China through the BRI deserves a historical and global look through the key insights from research on infrastructure in connection to state power.

The British state became the prototype of the modern infrastructure state in the early 18th century when it built a national network of roads to connect all towns and villages as far north as Scotland. It did so from a centralised bureaucratic apparatus in London by tearing down houses, measuring local roads and regulating distant surveyors. Despite its benefits such as improved transport of commercial goods and newspapers reaching the most remote villages, the nationalised road system led to isolated social relations and conflicts between the central and peripheral regions regarding payments for maintenance. As the

https://doi.org/10.1080/2578711X.2020.1823712

capitalist state expanded the realm of infrastructure construction to include railroads, bus lines, subways and public housing as in the 19th-century United States, it continued to push the poor to the urban edge and exclude poor regions from the more connected infrastructure system.[1] From the premise of a strong infrastructure–territoriality link, infrastructuring is a powerful strategy of the state to appropriate and control spaces as territoriality within its jurisdictional borders.[2] While globalisation may erode this state territorial strategy, it can enable and enhance it through transnational networks, allowing the historical version of the infrastructure state to function as a stronger and more globally oriented infrastructural state such as China.

Following this line of enquiry, we contend that the Chinese state acts not only as the strongest infrastructural state for its territory but also as the first one in history that builds out on a massive scale. It has built the world's largest system of infrastructure in the shortest period of time. Its global reach is reflected in having built and still building a variety of infrastructure projects, large or small, around the world. From how China has prioritised infrastructure in driving its domestic urbanisation and affecting urbanisation elsewhere, we see China's infrastructure power as shaping both embedded and connective infrastructure across the domestic–international divide. Inclusive of a range of urban and municipal facilities and services at the city level, infrastructure is central to the everyday experience of urban dwellers, especially in poor countries and cities where water, sanitation and waste facilities are severely underdeveloped.[3] Roads, railroads, airports, bridges, and telecommunication towers and lines combine into the connective infrastructure that carries circulations within cities and link flows among cities. Given the massive scale and key role of both embedded and connective infrastructures in China's domestic urbanisation, we first offer an overview of their salient features and processes to set up an analysis of how China influences urbanisation elsewhere through the infrastructure-heavy BRI.

3.3 CHINA'S URBANISATION: INFRASTRUCTURE AS THE KEY

Over the past four decades, China has transformed itself from a primarily rural and agrarian economy and society to a heavily urban and industrial one. By a widely used measure, 18% of China's total population lived in rural areas in 1978 and around 60% do so today. Over 600 million people have moved from villages into cities. China's urban population reached 830 million in 2018, more than four times that of 1978. In 2018 China had over 160 cities with over 1 million people, which accounted for 30% of all such cities in the world. This is compared with around 50 cities of this size in rapidly urbanising Africa, 35 in the entire Europe and only nine in the United States. China also had 33 (40%) of the 81 cities in the world with more

---

[1] Guidi J (2012) *Roads to Power: Britain Invents the Infrastructure State*. Cambridge, MA: Harvard University Press.
[2] Turner C (2020) *The Infrastructured State: Territoriality and the National Infrastructure System*. Cheltenham: Edward Elgar.
[3] Graham S and McFarlane C (eds.) (2015) *Infrastructural Lives: Urban Infrastructure in Context*. New York: Routledge.

than 5 million people.[4] These striking statistics demonstrate that China has urbanised at the fastest pace, on the largest scale and over the shortest time in human history.

China's urbanisation has produced generally beneficial economic and social outcomes. It was instrumental in lifting around 800 million people, predominantly in rural areas, out of extreme poverty. Chinese cities now account for 75% of national gross domestic product (GDP), which is projected to rise to 95% by 2025, while urban income has grown to three times that of rural income, from being roughly equal in 1978. China's urbanisation has also contributed positively to the global economy (Box 3.1).[5] China's urbanisation has been generally good for both China and the world.

Yet China's rapid and massive urbanisation has carried a few downsides. It has created a large spatial inequality between urban and rural areas and between the prosperous coastal cities and lagging interior and border regions. It has eaten up a lot of agricultural land through the expansion of built-up areas occupied by new industrial, commercial and residential construction. From 1997 to 2006, 12,869 km^2 of land were converted into built-up areas. During the same period, the average annual growth of built-up area in 135 cities was 5.7 km^2. This figure was much higher in larger cities. For example, Shenzhen added 66 km^2 of built-up area yearly on average.[6] Moreover, converting farmland, which has a carbon emission intensity of only 3 tons/km^2, into developed urban or industrial spaces drastically increased carbon emission intensity to 3364 or 4781 tons/km^2.[7] Furthermore, China has been the world's largest car market since 2009 and built over 130,000 km of highways, the longest in the world. This massive transport infrastructure has generated even more carbon emissions.

Both the beneficial and problematic outcomes of China's urbanisation have global dimensions, connections and repercussions. They run in both directions between China and the world. China has 'taken in' voluminous raw materials and commodities that are direct and indirect inputs into its city and infrastructure construction. As urbanisation has helped turn China from food self-sufficiency into a food importer due to the heavy loss of agricultural land and production, China has been meeting its growing demand for food by importing more agricultural products from neighbouring Kazakhstan and faraway Argentina.

> **Box 3.1   The power and benefits of China's urbanisation:**
>
> Chinese cities account for 75% of national gross domestic product (GDP) now and 95% by 2025
>
> China, primarily its urbanisation, accounted for 60% of global poverty reduction between 2005 and 2015
>
> Chinese cities will account for 30% of global urban consumption by 2030

---

[4] United Nations (2018) *The World's Cities in 2018*. Data Booklet. New York: United Nations.

[5] McKinsey (2009) *Preparing for China's Urban Billion*. New York: McKinsey Global Institute.

[6] Bai X, Chen J and Shi P (2012) Landscape urbanization and economic growth in China: Positive feedbacks and sustainability dilemmas. *Environmental Science and Technology*, 46(1): 132–139. Available online at: https://www.ncbi.nlm.nih.gov/pmc/articles/PMC3251221/.

[7] Li J and Xie P (2015) Urban China's appetite for land. *The Nature of Cities*, 20 May. Available online at: https://www.thenatureofcities.com/2015/05/20/urban-chinas-appetite-for-land/.

The insatiable consumption of cement and steel in constructing large cities and transport infrastructure has led China to source these commodities around the world, such as copper from Chile and Zambia and iron ore from Australia and Brazil. With 19% of the world's population and 18% of its GDP, China consumed 59% of the world's cement (dwarfing all other top national consumers) (Figure 3.1) and disproportionately large shares of other commodities (Box 3.2).[8] If China's 1 million plus cities will increase from 160 today to around 220 by 2030 as projected by McKinsey, China will need to build another 170 mass-transit systems, 40 billion m^2 of floor space and 50,000 more skyscrapers, the equivalent to constructing 10 New York cities from scratch. These would be needed as integral components of the future municipal and transport infrastructures to accommodate around 1 billion urbanites.[9]

> **Box 3.2 China's dominant consumption of the world's commodities with about 18% of the world's population and about 19% of the world's gross domestic product (GDP), China consumes:**
>
> 59% of the world's cement
>
> 50% of the world's copper
>
> 50% of the world's steel
>
> 47% of the world's pork

Figure 3.1   Major countries in worldwide cement production, 2014–18 (millions of tons)

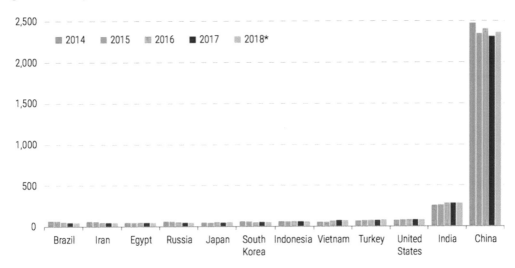

Note: *2018 data estimatedSources: Pinebridge Investments, Statista; US Geological Surveys

To reveal the essence of China's urbanisation, its speeding and scaling are striking. With less than 20% of its population living in urban areas in 1980, China was behind India at 23% and Africa as a whole at around 20%. China has left them far behind and reached a level of urbanisation at 60% compared with 40% for Africa and 35% for India. China completed 77 of the world's 144 new supertall buildings with

---

[8] *Visual Capitalist* (2018) China's staggering demand for commodities. *Visual Capitalist*, 2 March. Available online at: www.visualcapitalist.com/chinas-staggering-demand-commodities/.

[9] McKinsey (2009); see Reference 5.

a minimum height of 200 m across 36 different cities in 2017 compared with 113 buildings of this height in New York City.[10] The Chinese state has steered urbanisation at an unprecedented speed and scale. Moreover, this steering has accelerated and scaled up both embedded infrastructure in cities and connective infrastructure among cities.

Since 2014, when the government unveiled a new vision on urbanisation, speeding and scaling have given away to efficiency, inclusivity and sustainability. This shift has slowed the largely saturated domestic construction market and created a strong push behind China 'building out' into the world. The overcapacity of steel, cement and other construction materials has provided another impetus to building overseas. Having accumulated much engineering expertise from building large-scale infrastructure projects domestically, China's state-owned construction enterprises have extended their reach and capacity to build infrastructure internationally, again at a fast pace and on a large scale. As we move from the domestic inside to understand the global outside of China's impact on urbanisation via the BRI, we hold the state–urban relationship as the analytical key and examine how it works through the following case study.

3.4 BUILDING OUT: BORTEN ON THE CHINA–LAOS BORDER

Building large-scale infrastructure in developing countries is not new for China, which constructed the Tanzania–Zambia Railway between 1970 and 1975 for US$406 million (the equivalent of US$2.62 billion today), China's single largest foreign-aid project at the time. What has changed is that China's construction in developing countries has recently gone far beyond the traditional national development assistance arena and shifted increasingly to projects for improving municipal and transport infrastructure supporting urban and industrial development. Two examples illustrate this broad shift. One is the light rail system in Addis Ababa, the capital city of Ethiopia, built by China and in operation since 2015. Consisting of two lines covering 31.6 km with 40 stations; the tram serves riders between the city centre and the industrial areas south of the city. The second example is China's comprehensive role in building power stations, airports, hospitals, commercial facilities and residential buildings in and around Cambodia's top cities of Phnom Penh and Sihanoukville.[11] In both contexts, China-built infrastructure combines embedded and connective elements that serve municipal needs and facilitate extra-local mobilities.[12]

To understand China's broad role in shaping urbanisation in developing countries, we reiterate Shenzhen as the starting place and sustained template of China's infrastructure build-out. In leading China's first geographical turn (Table 1.1), Shenzhen became an 'instant city' as it rose from a small village and spatially

---

[10] *Visual Capitalist* (2018); see Reference 8.

[11] *Go Out Information Bulletin* (2019) Chinese SOEs secured 20 new large infrastructure projects in Cambodia in 2019. *Go Out Information Bulletin*, 22 November. Available online at: https://mp.weixin.qq.com/s/U3Za8j73MzVBG5Iwt5A_VQ.

[12] Chen X and Stone C (2017) Rethinking border cities: In-between spaces, unequal actors and stretched mobilities across the China–Southeast Asia borderland. In S Hall and R Burdett (eds.), *The SAGE Handbook of the 21st Century City*, pp. 479–501. Thousand Oaks, CA: Sage.

cordoned SEZ with fewer than 100,000 people bordering Hong Kong into a megacity of around 15 million including temporary residents in fewer than four decades. Fuelling this demographic explosion was the dramatic spatial transformation of agricultural fields into a hyper-urban and ultramodern landscape of industrial parks, residential towers, shopping malls and transport infrastructure, amounting to the quadruple nature or content of China's infrastructure-led city building. Besides its exemplary role in leading China's domestic urbanisation, Shenzhen's spirit and practice have moved toward and beyond China's other land borders. The small Chinese cities of Ruili bordering Myanmar and Khorgos bordering Kazakhstan have appropriated traces of Shenzhen in creating their own SEZs. Large old cities in western China such as Xi'an have looked east to young Shenzhen's development as a model for renewing their industrial systems and forging new beneficial transborder connections such as the CEFT (see chapter 2).

Corridors 1–3 of the BRI have created new overland trade and logistical connectivities that run in the west direction along three CEFT routes (Figures 1.1 and 2.1). Corridor 4, which runs north–south along China–Indochina Peninsular corridor (Figure 1.1; and see Box 1.1), has carried China's strong inside-out influence on infrastructure-led urbanisation based on the Shenzhen template. We now turn to this corridor to reveal China's growing but still somewhat under-recognised role in shaping urbanisation beyond its borders. While all BRI corridors originate from China, the China–Indochina Peninsular corridor starts from Kunming, the capital of Yunnan province and the dominant economic hub for south-western China, similar to Xi'an as both a key departing and return point for the CEFT.

More specifically, we focus on the Laotian town of Borten opposite the Chinese town of Mohan across the China–Laos border as our case for understanding China's overseas construction of a new city with embedded urban infrastructure. We then move north to Kunming and farther south to Vientiane, the capital of Laos, to examine the CLR as a connective infrastructure project. The coupling of both cases defines the length and key contents of the China–Laos economic corridor, a sub-corridor of the BRI's Corridor 4 (Figure 1.1).

3.4.1 A new city as embedded infrastructure

A small and sleepy rural village nestled in the agricultural fields surround by mountains covered by tropical forests in the backwater of northern Laos, Borten remained poor and largely isolated through the 1990s, despite being designated as a first-class land port by the Laotian government in 1993, when Mohan was also granted the same designation. Fast forward 10 years to 2003, a Hong Kong-registered company signed a 30-year lease with the Laotian government to set up an SEZ of 16.4 km^2 known as Borten Golden City. Despite its goal of promoting trade and tourism, the Borten zone ended as a den of gambling that provided easy visa-free access to wealthy gamblers from China where gambling has always been illegal.[13]

---

[13] Strangio S (2016) The rise, fall and possible renewal of a town in Laos on China's border. *The New York Times*, 6 July. Available online at: https://www.nytimes.com/2016/07/07/world/asia/china-laos-Borten-gambling.html.

Other Chinese came to the border on buses from Kunming and beyond as tourists who would travel on to tourist cities such as Luang Prabang in northern Laos. They could swap the Chinese currency of yuan for the Laotian currency of kip freely. Lao locals in Borten who could speak Chinese offered car services and peddled cheap goods. Such gambling-related problems as money laundering and prostitution led the Chinese government to pressure Laos to close the casinos and it left Borten like a 'ghost town'.[14]

Borten turned to better fortune in 2009 when the Laotian government designated it as a new SEZ to be independently operated, but under central government supervision. Yet little happened until 2015 when the Chinese and Laotian governments signed the Agreement for Joint Construction of the China–Laos Borten–Mohan Economic Cooperation Zone (ECZ). In 2016, the two governments agreed on a master plan for jointly developing the ECZ, which covers 21.2 km^2, with 16.4 km^2 in Borten and 4.8 km^2 in Mohan. While the Chinese side would focus on building for and attracting regional corporate headquarters, the still independent Borten SEZ would focus on developing four subzones specialised in: (1) international commerce and finance, (2) international duty-free logistics and assembly, (3) international education and medical industry and (4) international services. These specialised functions would be integrated into a comprehensive new city with residential housing for 300,000 people working and living locally (Figure 3.2). Like the CEFT, which began in 2011, predated the BRI and has been its prominent part since 2013, the Borten project has been incorporated into or claimed by the BRI since 2013.

Figure 3.2   The Borten special economic zone/New Border City under construction

Source: Promotional photograph from Yunnan Haicheng Industry Group Co., with permission

---

[14]Chen X (2019) Change and continuity in special economic zones: A reassessment and lessons from China. *Transnational Corporations*, 26(2): 49–74.

                https://doi.org/10.1080/2578711X.2020.1823712

While the Borten SEZ is being built into a new city, it offers a set of familiar and generous financial incentives. These include: (1) the exemption of import duties for all goods and materials used, sold and served in the zone; (2) 5% value-added tax, 5% payroll tax and 0–10% profit tax for all factories in the zone; (3) reduction or exemption of profit tax for 3–10 years for investors; and (4) the made-in-Laos permit and tariff-free exports to third countries. These incentives have been operationalised into the so-called 'One-Stop Shopping' to facilitate speedy and efficient approval of investment projects (Figure 3.3). This way of organising the incentives is simi-

Figure 3.3 Borten special economic zone 'one-stop' service centre

Source: Lead author

lar to what the Shenzhen SEZ offered at its early stage of development, before it became a fully fledged city. While it is unlikely that Borten will ever reach Shenzhen's scale and complexity, it is emerging as a new or 'instant' city inspired by the Shenzhen template. It is clear that Borten's short and 'miraculous' history will be enshrined in a new urban planning exhibition centre under construction.

The Borten SEZ is a major BRI project on the China–Indochina Peninsular Corridor (number 4 in Figure 1.1) and represents embedded infrastructure in the form of a new city. Symbolising the city's BRI-oriented ambition is an international finance centre in a cluster of 20-storey towers and a 30-plus-storey International Trade Centre. While this symbolic and functional prominence appears unnecessary for a relatively small new city, it reflects the construction expertise and business motive of Haicheng, a private real estate development company headquartered in Kunming where it has built a large amount of commercial and residential properties, and in the broader region extending south to the border. In bidding to build Borten, Haicheng beat its competitors because of its commercial influence in the regional market and strong connections with the prefectural government on the Chinese side of the order.[15] Since 2016, Haicheng has been building the Borten SEZ on a 90-year land lease. It has already invested around US$1 billion, completed 80% of land clearance, 258,526 m^2 of commercial and residential real estate (78% of which has been under contract), and is planning to invest a total of US$10 billion and complete the project over 10–15 years.[16]

Much of Haicheng's investment in Borten has come from bank loans made by the China–Laos Bank, a joint venture between a Laotian state bank and the Yunnan Fudian Bank. Since the Laotian government itself has little to invest in building up Borten, Haicheng has footed the bulk of the financing and begun to partner

---

[15] Interview with an informant who has worked for Haicheng on both sides of the border.
[16] Xinhua (2019) *Laos' Special Economic Zone Bordering China to Lure 10 bln USD Investment*. Xinhua, 28 October. Available at: www.xinhuanet.com/english/2019-10/28/c_138510459.htm.

with other private Chinese and Laotian companies for the construction and commercial projects. However, Haicheng has struggled financially and sometimes been unable to pay its subcontractors as its properties remain partially sold.[17] Yet it has served as the dominant player in building up a critical project for the BRI, thus softening the political image of the BRI as a state-driven initiative. In return, Haicheng has benefited from the political wind unleashed by the BRI in advancing its business into neighbouring Laos. Given its financial heft and the weak Laotian government, Haicheng also plays a key role in Borten's governance structure in partnership with a Laotian agency. The company's prominent role in building and governing a new Laotian city points to both a blurring and collaboration between the BRI as China's dominant economic foreign policy and Chinese private capital's pursuit of profits in an overseas construction market to offset the saturated and dwindling domestic property market.

As additional evidence on Chinese's private sector involvement in building and enhancing embedded infrastructure in Borten as a new city, a private healthcare company (Jinxin Medical Group) with hospitals in China has recently acquired the first medical facility in Borten, the Rhea International Medical Centre, and plans to upgrade it to anticipate and accommodate the need to deal with COVID-19 patients. Jinxin has also donated medical supplies worth of US$20 million to Luang Namtha province, of which Borten is part, in northern Laos to fight COVID-19.[18] Influenced by the BRI or not, an unprecedented public health crisis has created new private–public partnerships that bridge and mitigate healthcare disparities as part of new urbanisation across borders. It prompts us to think about how the private and public sectors can cooperate better in building more balanced and well-rounded infrastructure that characterises the BRI's priorities and practices.

3.4.2 An ambitious railway as connective infrastructure

Located in the isolated mountainous region in Laos, a landlocked and least developed country in Southeast Asia, the Borten SEZ is incapable of generating much agglomeration or spillovers despite its audacious start as a new city. Its location, however, has turned out to be a natural and planned advantage in external connectivity through the ambitious CLR. Originating from Kunming and travelling across the border all the way south to the Laotian capital of Vientiane, the CLR passes through the cities of Yuxi and Puer in Yunnan province, Mohan and Borten in the border zone, and then runs past Luang Prabang and Vang Vieng before arriving in Vientiane (Figure 3.4).

While the idea for the CLR project germinated in 2010, it was not until December 2015 that both governments broke ground for construction. The timing clearly corresponded with the joint agreement to establish the China–Laos ECZ. Designed to carry both cargo and passengers, the electric railway will run at an average speed of 160 km/h, which qualifies it as high-to-medium speed. The Laotian government expects

---

[17] See Reference 15.
[18] The Borten SEZ's electronic newsletter, 24 April 2020.

Figure 3.4   The China–Laos railway in a regional context

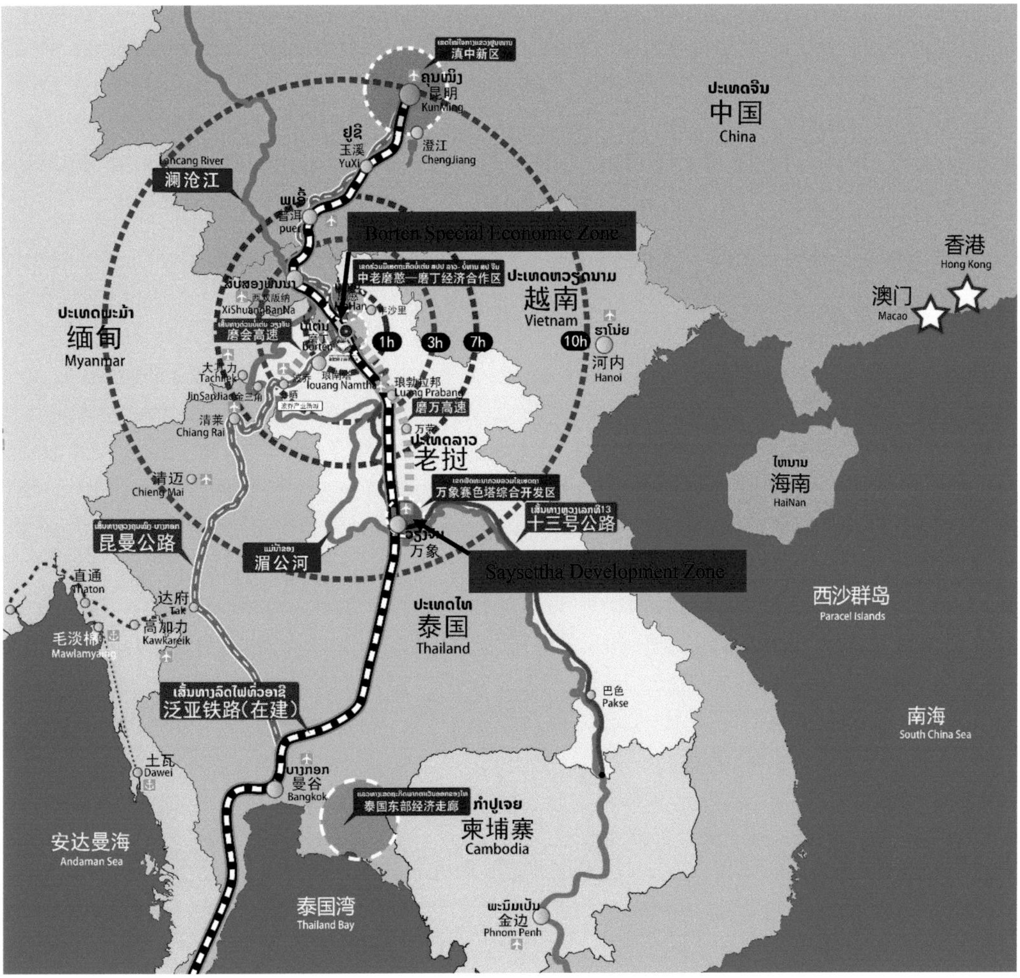

Source: Same as Figure 3.2, with the legends of the Borten and Saysettha zones added by lead author.

around 4 million Laotian passengers a year to use the railway's 420-km route through the country at first, growing to 6.1 million passengers in the mid-term and to 8.1 million passengers later on.[19] The CLR defines and anchors the backbone of the China–Laos corridor, a sub-corridor of the BRI's Corridor 4 (Figure 1.1).

This projected large economic payoff from heavy cross-border travel does not come cheaply. To finance the project cost of US$6 billion relative to Laos' annual GDP of US$12 billion, Laos has borrowed 60%, or US$3.5 billion, in low-interest loans from the Export and Import Bank of China

---

[19] Radio Free Asia (2016) Laos and China come to terms on loan interest rate for railway project. Radio Free Asia, 4 January. Available at: http://www.rfa.org/english/news/laos/China-Laos-come-to-terms-on-loan-interest-rate-for-railway-project-01042016163552.html.

(EximBank).[20] Heavily and prominently financed by EximBank, the CLR elevates the bank's profile as one of the main financial sources for the BRI's large-scale infrastructure projects (see chapter 1). Unlike Borten, financed primarily by the private development company of Haicheng, the strong financing from powerful sources like EximBank steers the bulk of the construction work to China's large state-owned railroad companies led by China Railway Group Ltd (CREC), one of the world's largest construction and engineering contractors, which ranked 56th among Fortune Global 500 in 2018. The project also involves the specialised participation of other Chinese construction and engineering state-owned enterprises (SOEs).

With extensive technical expertise and excellent equipment from home, the Chinese railroad companies have been on track to finish the CLR on time by December 2021. They work around the clock to lay tracks through tunnels and over elevated bridges, which make up 60% of the route's length. This includes 93 tunnels and 136 elevated bridges just for the section between Yuxi and Mohan on the border (Figure 3.4). On 13 March 2020, all work for and through the 17.4 km-long Wanhe Tunnel near Yuxi was completed. This most difficult control project along the southern Yunnan section of the CLR required the collaboration among rail engineering and hydropower drilling SOEs at both national and provincial levels. On 27 March 2020, the first track at the station in Vientiane was laid to mark symbolically the railway's southern terminus.

On 29 April 2020, a ceremony was held in Vientiane to mark the beginning of the building of all the rail stations on the Laos side. These are markers of progress after a full return to construction after COVID-19, which 'seriously affected' about one-fifth of all BRI projects.[21] Once completed, the train will be able to reach Borten from Vientiane in three hours instead of the two days on the current road. It will allow Laos to use Borten as Laos' largest trucking logistics station and outlet (Figure 3.5) for exporting 90% of its bananas, the country's largest export. (China also happens to be the overall largest export market for Laos.) By speeding up both freight and passenger mobilities within and across

Figure 3.5   Logistics yard at the Mohan–Borten border

Source: The Borten WeChat public platform, with permission

---

[20] Chen X (2018) Globalization redux: Can China's inside-out strategy catalyze economic development across its Asian borderlands and beyond? *Cambridge Journal of Regions, Economy and Society*, 11(1), 35–58.

[21] Reuters (2020) China says one-fifth of Belt and Road projects 'seriously affected' by pandemic. Reuters, 18 June. Available at: https://uk.reuters.com/article/uk-health-coronavirus-china-silkroad/china-says-one-fifth-of-belt-and-road-projects-seriously-affected-by-pandemic-idUKKBN23Q0HZ?il=0.

the China–Southeast Asia borderlands, the CLR embodies the power of the Chinese infrastructure state in connecting the embedded and connective infrastructures.[22]

The CLR as a massive connective infrastructure project aims to turn landlocked Laos and its 'disconnected destiny' to land- and sea-linked as there is a plan to extend the railway from Vientiane to Bangkok, Thailand, and then all the way to Singapore via Malaysia, with access to the sea via both Bangkok and Singapore. The new Vientiane–Borten highway, once linked up with the Kunming–Mohan highway at the border, will provide a direct connection for northern Laos to access the sea from Bangkok along the Kunming–Bangkok highway (Figure 3.4). Anticipating the trade benefit from access to the sea, China and Laos in June 2010 signed a memorandum of understanding (MOU) to build the Saysettha Development Zone (SDZ) near the planned railway freight station in Vientiane from which products from the zone can be easily shipped out. With the state-owned China Merchants Group (CMG) as a main investor (also see chapter 4), the zone aims to attract around 150 enterprises to operate there to generate an output of US$6 billion and about 30,000 new jobs by 2030. By 2018, some 47 companies from China, Laos, Thailand and Singapore have already moved into the zone, with an aggregate investment of more than US$500 million.[23] If this is evidence on the potential multiplier effect of the connective infrastructure in Vientiane, it offers hope for the new Borten SEZ in the much less developed northern Laos to benefit from the CLR to access the sea and maritime trade. As the pandemic elevated the Association of Southeast Asian Nations (ASEAN) to replace the European Union as China's largest trading partner in the first quarter of 2020, the coupling of the Borten and CLR projects heralds a stronger China–ASEAN economic nexus through new land–sea trade ties.

3.5 IN THE SHADOW OF INFRASTRUCTURE-LED URBANISATION

From the Borten SEZ/new city to the CLR, China has been building infrastructure embedded in a new city in northern Laos and connecting it to major capital cities within and beyond Laos in Southeast Asia along a new cross-country railway. While this combination promises to accelerate urbanisation in Laos, it may come at a considerable cost and with potential downsides to the hosting nation. Since the railway's cost is half of Laos' small GDP, pessimistic government officials worry that Laos will be plagued with the risk of high debt and budgetary crisis after the project is completed.

---

[22]Lampton D M, Ho S and Kuik C-C (2020) *Rivers of Iron: Railroads and Chinese Power in Southeast Asia*. Berkeley, CA: University of California Press.

[23]*Vientiane Times* (2018) Chinese developer gives boost to Saysettha Development Zone. *Vientiane Times*, 4 August. Available at: https://annx.asianews.network/content/chinese-developer-gives-boost-saysettha-development-zone-78385.

For landlocked Laos, this railway makes sense for connecting to outside markets, especially if the Borten SEZ and SDZ near Vientiane's terminal can stimulate manufactured exports, and if millions of high-spending Chinese tourists cross the border by train. However, a feasibility study performed by a Chinese company revealed that the railway would lose money for the first 11 years.[24] In the meantime, some Laotian farmers have been denied sufficient government compensation for giving up their land for the railway. China has brought over equipment and the main prefabricated parts for the rail project (Figure 3.6). At peak construction before COVID-19, there were an estimated 100,000 Chinese workers along the rail route. While China has benefited from this megaproject by putting its surplus construction materials and labour to work, there has been relatively little subcontracting or spillover of material processing and production for Laotian companies and thus limited employment for Laotian workers.

Figure 3.6 China-fabricated rail tracks trucked through the Borten border

Source: Lead author

Finally, as a China-built new city inside Laos, Borten has thus far attracted mostly Chinese corporate and individual investors who have purchased the bulk of the completed commercial and residential properties. This raises the critical question of why and how Borten can avoid becoming an exclusive space only for Chinese investors and residents while keeping out Laotian citizens. This scenario is more likely considering that the Chinese private development company building Borten is heavily involved in local governance. In this kind of large-scale infrastructure construction by a powerful outsider, local 'others' can be easily absent and excluded by what is included.[25] This can lead to the erosion of political and territorial sovereignty and governance of the countries hosting China-funded SEZs such as Laos. The involvement of Chinese state and private companies in building urban and connective infrastructure overseas reflects the growing diversity and complexity of actors and agencies in China's overall global engagement. It posts challenges to all policy-makers in national and local governments, planning agencies and the construction sector who face and work with the BRI in shaping global urbanisation through infrastructure construction.

---

[24] Chen (2018); see Reference 20.

[25] Wigg A and Silver J (2019) Turbulent presents, precarious futures: Urbanization and the deployment of global infrastructure. *Regional Studies*, 53(6): 912–923.

3.6 SUMMARY AND POLICY RECOMMENDATIONS

As the largest and fastest urbanising nation in history, China has become the world's foremost builder of a full range of infrastructure undergirding and connecting its expanding cities. China's urbanisation slowed over time and ran much of its course eventually, leading China to 'export' infrastructure construction as a critical strategy for implementing the BRI. This has turned China into a powerful urbanising force and the BRI into a contributor to global urbanisation. Through a case study of Laos' border town of Borten, we have demonstrated how China, through a regional private development company (Haicheng), has built a new city with its entire embedded infrastructure. We have also examined the CLR as a large-scale connective infrastructure project built by China to link Borten to larger cities along the railway on both sides of the border.

To the extent that infrastructure construction defines a distinctive and continuing stage of China-led globalisation (Table 2.1), it manifests itself most intensively and extensively in China's building of new cities and transport systems to link them. The China State Construction Engineering Corporation has been building a 20-tower central business district as part of Egypt's new capital about 50 km east of Cairo, with a 385 m-high 80-floor iconic tower that will be the tallest building in Egypt and Africa upon completion. In a similar project, the Shanghai Construction Group is building a trio of tall towers to house Uzbekistan's top state-owned banks. These buildings will anchor and symbolise the new financial district overshadowing the surrounding Soviet-era low-rise buildings in the heart of Tashkent, the capital. China Railway International is the main builder of the Jakarta–Bandung High-Speed Railway, financed primarily by the National Development Bank (China) as another major funder of BRI projects (see chapter 1) and 60% completed. Designed to cover 150 km and run at 200–250 km/h, this new railway will carry an average of 44,000 passengers daily and cut the travel time between Indonesia's two central hubs from the original 3–5 hours to less than 40 minutes. The main stations in both cities will link to a light-rail system connecting their airports.

Augmented by these examples, our combined analysis of Borten new city and the CLR invokes lessons for policy-makers at the international, national and local levels from the practice and impact of China's overseas urban and infrastructure construction (Box 3.3).

Box 3.3   Policy recommendations for the BRI versus urbanisation:

- We recommend policies for better coordination between the central and local governments of countries receiving or hosting Chinese-built new cities and transport projects. These policies should encourage national governments to negotiate, bargain and approve China's construction projects in a transparent manner and to empower relatively weak local governments to have a bigger say on the terms and feasibility of projects sited in their jurisdictions
- We strongly advocate policies for both China and developing host countries to enforce environmental standards and green-land preservation and to avoid the unnecessary loss of agricultural land and the ecosystem to rapid urbanisation as happened within China

---

- In connection with the above point, we encourage better policies to guide developing countries and cities in balancing Chinese-built new urban and connective infrastructure with the uneven demographic distribution, large informal settlements and uncontrolled migration in their systems. It is critical to prioritise secondary or regional centres and key transport links to redress the primate-city syndrome of crowded living and insufficient basic services as water and sanitation in capital or largest cities
- We need policies to promote stronger indigenous governance for new cities and management of large-scale transport projects. It is mutually beneficial to accord a greater role in governing Borten new city to the Laotian government. It is also critical to sustain China's training of local workers and engineers to operate transport systems sustainably as what China has done in Africa (see chapter 4).

https://doi.org/10.1080/2578711X.2020.1823712

4. THE BRI AND DEVELOPMENT

4.1 INTRODUCTION

Having examined the BRI's impacts on globalisation and urbanisation through forging connectivities and building infrastructure, respectively, we turn to the third leg of this book's framework by looking at how the BRI is also reshaping the landscape of economic development on an increasing global scale (Figure 1.5). The two preceding chapters feed logically into this one, because the BRI-created new connectivities and infrastructures across regional and national boundaries generate previously unavailable opportunities for national and local development. While trade connection and transport infrastructure can facilitate development through export-oriented manufacturing, the ways by which this positive impact or potential undesirable consequences are channelled need to be scrutinised.

In this chapter we first recast the notion of development by connecting the United Nations' (UN) Development Goals and the BRI. We then investigate how China has impacted African development through the BRI by: (1) (re)building Djibouti Port following the template of Shekou in Shenzhen; (2) fostering light manufacturing in Ethiopia in China-built special economic zones (SEZs) that also trace back to Shenzhen; and (3) spurring corridor-shaped regional development by linking landlocked Ethiopia to Djibouti via a new cross-border railway as the China–Laos Railway (CLR). We also highlight the combined and complementary roles of the China Merchants Group (CMG) as a global state-owned enterprise (SOE) and a large and global private company such as Huajian that shed a light on the hidden state–private nexus in the BRI.

4.2 RECASTING DEVELOPMENT: ALIGNING THE UNITED NATIONS' DEVELOPMENT GOALS AND THE BRI

To assess the BRI's impact on development beyond China, we must again look at how China itself has developed for useful cross-national lessons in policy and practice. This, however, is not sufficient unless we take another look at how the concept of development has shifted in the broader context of the UN's Millennium Development Goals (MDGs) for 2015 and Sustainable Development Goals (SDGs) for 2030, which shed a light on China's own development experience and its relevance for other developing countries via the BRI.

As the concept of development has received considerable reassessment, China's economic miracle over the past four decades shines a spotlight on the question of how one country's successful development is adaptable or transferrable to others lower on the development ladder. It has been recognised by now that development is more than economic growth, although the latter is the essential engine of development. In the year 2000, the UN's Millennium Declaration envisioned development broadly to comprise eight goals to combat poverty, hunger, disease, illiteracy, environmental degradation and discrimination against women.[1]

---

[1] The eight Millennium Development Goals (MDGs) are: (1) eradicate extreme poverty and hunger; (2) achieve universal primary education; (3) promote gender equality and empower women; (4) reduce child mortality; (5) improve maternal health; (6) combat HIV/AIDS, malaria and other diseases; (7) ensure environmental sustainability; and (8) develop a global partnership for development.

https://doi.org/10.1080/2578711X.2020.1823715

Known as MDGs, they set targets for 2015 based on indicators to monitor progress from 1990 levels. The first and primary MDG, for example, aimed to cut the 1990 poverty rate by half while taking into account adjusted minimum income levels of extreme poverty.

Despite the mixed and uneven progress with rapid poverty reduction in China and increased extreme poverty in Sub-Saharan Africa by the mid-2000s, the goal was generally achieved by 2010, ahead of the 2015 target. As the first country to reach this goal, China accounted for 76% of the global poverty reduction as its (extreme) poverty ratio dropped from around 70% in 1990 to 1.85% in 2013, which translated into over 750 million people.[2]

While rapid economic growth and poverty reduction have run together in China, development has taken a very unbalanced and volatile path in countries such as Equatorial Guinea. With the discovery of oil in 1996, per capita income in Equatorial Guinea rose from US$1970 in 2000 to US$20,246 in 2013, before falling to US$8333 in 2016 (and staying in the upper middle income group; see Appendix A). Yet Equatorial Guinea's social indicators did not improve with its oil wealth as its life expectancy remained under 60 years in 2016.[3] In comparison, poorer countries such as Ethiopia (still in the low income category; see Appendix A) raised its life expectancy from 46.9 years in 1990 to 66.3 years in 2018. China is more telling over a longer period. After doubling its life expectancy from around 35 years in 1949 to 66.8 years in 1980, under a socialist planned economy and at a very low level of development, China's life expectancy rose further to 76.8 years in 2018.[4] This comparative evidence reveals oil as a natural resource curse for Equatorial Guinea, the lack of synchronisation between economic development and health improvement in Ethiopia, and a broader and more balanced sequence of sustainable development in China.

In hindsight, the timing for the BRI's official inauguration in 2013 and the unveiling of the UN's 2030 Agenda for Sustainable Development in 2015 may be more than coincidental. This agenda has advanced 17 SDGs,[5] which further broaden the meaning and scope of development. The key to achieving these SDGs is to pursue global development and 'win–win' cooperation, which can bring big gains to all countries and all parts of the world. Not coincidentally, the BRI has been touted as creating 'win–win' opportunities for international relations and economic development.[6] The Chinese government has sold the BRI as a way to revitalise global partnership for development and implement the 2030 Agenda. It has cited the large number of signed international cooperation agreements in the BRI framework as evidence that the UN's SDGs and the BRI can be mutually beneficial. To show that China-driven cooperative development via the BRI goes beyond trade and investment, the Chinese government has provided 290 training courses for

---

[2] Tang W (2018) *China's Approach to Reduce Poverty: Taking Targeted Measures to Lift People Out of Poverty*. Addis Ababa: International Poverty Reduction Center in China.

[3] Goldin I (2018) *Development: A Very Short Introduction*. New York: Oxford University Press.

[4] Macrotrends (2020) *Life Expectancy 1950–2020*. Available at: www.macrotrends.net/countries/.

[5] The 17 SDGs are listed on the UN's knowledge platform. Available online at: https://sustainabledevelopment.un.org/post2015/transformingourworld.

[6] Xinhua (2019) *Interview: China-Proposed BRI Creates Win–Win Fair Model for Int'l Relations: Egyptian Expert*. Xinhua, 12 December. Available at: www.xinhuanet.com/english/2019-12/10/c_138621126.htm.

5487 participants from 133 developing countries and territories as of March 2019.[7] As human capital and skills enhancement help sustain long-run development, the BRI can contribute to the achievement of the UN's SDGs.

China has contributed to global development by providing other social assistance such as medical teams in African countries before and through the BRI. Yet China's strongest influence on development has always been manufacturing, which earned China the moniker 'Factory of the World'. The BRI allows China to play that role in international development by extending its accumulated advantages and expertise in building and scaling industrial production with supportive infrastructure. China's ability to provide varied infrastructure to developing countries (see chapter 3) distinguishes its role in international development. This connection crystalises in China-built SEZs for hosting new factories to make products, primarily for export markets. It signifies a sort of policy mobility of development practices from China to the developing world, which will yield evidence and insights on the success, or lack of it, beyond case studies in policy mobility generally conducted in the Western context.[8] We have a test case in Djibouti below.

The BRI's shift toward a more balanced and selective orientation toward both infrastructure and trade and investment through the so-called BRI 2.0 since the second BRI Forum in April 2019 has reinforced an emphasis on manufacturing projects. Africa stands out in hosting SEZs in cooperation with Chinese government and private company investments. This development provides lasting localised assets that foster economic development in Africa.[9] It harkens back to China's own success in coupling urbanisation and industrialisation to create sustainable economic development, which in turn has led to broader social development.

4.3 BUILDING AFRICA'S INDUSTRIAL LANDSCAPE

From a development vantage point, no other region links China's experience to indigenous conditions better than Africa. Looking for a part of Africa that best reveals a potential adaptation of China's development experience, we leave the BRI's land-based corridors to focus on a key segment of the Maritime Silk Road and its broader hinterland or neighbourhood – the Horn of Africa between the Indian Ocean and the Red Sea, and the larger region of East Africa. To be consistent with the earlier cases of the China–Europe freight corridor and the China–Laos corridor, we construct this chapter's case into a corridor-shaped development space anchored by Djibouti (and its capital city of Djibouti City) and Ethiopia (and its capital city of Addis Ababa). This corridor is (re)joined by and anchored to the China-built Addis Ababa–Djibouti Railway (ADR), which was inaugurated and went into commercial operation on 1 January 2018 (Figure 4.1). Like the

---

[7] Ministry of Foreign Affairs (2019) *China's Progress Report on Implementation of the 2030 Agenda for Sustainable Development*. Beijing: Ministry of Foreign Affairs.

[8] McCann E and Ward K (eds.) (2011) *Mobile Urbanism: Cities and Policy-Making in a Global Age*. Minneapolis: University of Minnesota Press.

[9] Sun I Y (2017) *The Next Factory of the World: How Chinese Investment is Reshaping Africa*. Cambridge, MA: Harvard Business Review Press.

Figure 4.1   The Djibouti (Djibouti City)–Ethiopia (Addis Ababa) Development Corridor

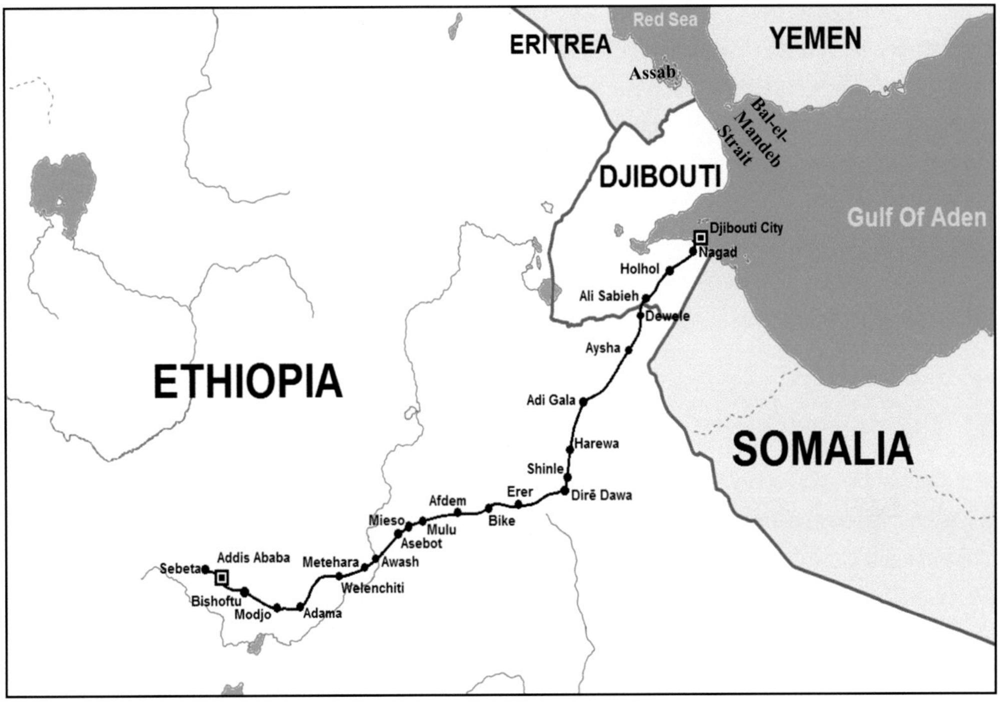

Source: Wikimedia Commons, no permission needed

CLR, the ADR joins both freight and passenger lines. This not only makes rail connection central to all three case studies (see chapters 2–4) but also creates continuity from the China–Laos corridor featuring the relationship between urbanisation (the Borten new border city) and infrastructure-induced development associated with the CLR. We also see a parallel between the tackling of the landlocked and no land–sea connection barriers for both Laos and Ethiopia.

We take Djibouti as the place of departure for our analysis. Located on the Gulf of Aden and bordered by Somalia, Ethiopia and Eritrea on three sides, Djibouti sits at the crossroads of the shipping route between the Indian Ocean and the Mediterranean Sea through the Red Sea and the Suez Canal, most critically through the narrow Bal-el-Mandeb Strait separating Yemen and Djibouti (Figure 4.1). This geostrategic chokepoint saw the transit of 6.2 million barrels per day (bpd) of crude oil, condensate and refined petroleum products towards Europe, the United States and Asia in 2018. The oil flow through this strait pales in comparison with the much larger flows of 19 million bpd through the Strait of Hormuz and 16 million bpd through the Strait of Malacca in 2016.[10] Nevertheless, the Bal-el-Mandeb Strait is a critically important gateway for maritime trade between Asia and Africa and Europe and North America through the Suez Canal.

---

[10] Raga A A (2020) *The Bab-el-Mandeb strait: Geopolitical considerations of the strategic chokepoint*. Opinion Paper, 10 March. Madrid: Institutto Español de Estudio Estratégicos (IEEE).

Djibouti's location in the heart of this region raises its importance to the world and China, which imported one-third of its crude oil from Saudi Arabia, Iraq, Oman, the Gulf countries and members of the Organization of the Petroleum Exporting Countries (OPEC) in 2018. For these and other reasons, including the establishment of China's first overseas naval base near Djibouti City's deep-water port in 2017, which sits in close proximity to the American, French and Japanese military bases, research on this region, and Djibouti in particular, has adopted a primarily geostrategic focus on broad military and security issues.[11] It overshadows China's quiet and grounded activities in Djibouti, capital city of Djibouti, and its port that can reveal a lot about how intensively China has been reshaping economic development in Africa. We take a focused look at China's local influence in Djibouti through a mode of development that can be traced to a small locality in southern China four decades ago.

4.3.1 The 'port–park–city' (PPC) mode of development: from Shekou to Djibouti

Due to the combination of being a small city and having a disproportionately more important port, Djibouti City has become an experimental ground for China to introduce the so-called 'port–park–city' (PPC) mode[12] of development pioneered by the Shekou industrial zone that seeded the take-off of the Shenzhen SEZ in 1979. Two-thirds of Djibouti's population of around 900,000 over 23,200 km^2 are concentrated or crowded into the city's 26 km^2 urban area.[13] Despite being surrounded by a much larger and underdeveloped national hinterland with few natural resources, Djibouti City's deep-water port offers shipping connections to and from other important ports and markets in the immediate region and further afield.

Although the Djibouti port area was a point of maritime contact and exploration near the Red Sea for ancient peoples, including the Greeks, Romans and Arabs, for over three millennia, the actual port function did not develop until 1879 when French colonialists began to build the old Ethio-Djibouti Railway in order to give landlocked Ethiopia access to the sea. The railway's completion in 1917 accelerated the port's growth, although its activity remained somewhat limited and confined to bulk cargo through the 1970s. With its first container terminal starting operation in 1985, Djibouti Port developed into a regional port with some transhipping functions between the Red Sea and Indian Ocean and beyond.[14] Yet the port's potential larger scale and geographical reach were underachieved until the 21st century with China's growing local presence and influence.

[11] Cabestan J-P (2019) China's military base in Djibouti: A microcosm of China's growing competition with the United States and new bipolarity. *Journal of Contemporary China*, 29(125): 731–747. doi:10.1080/10670564.2019.1704994.
[12] We prefer the word 'mode' to 'model' for labelling the particular way of sequencing the (re)construction of a port, an industrial park, and a new city in the small locality and distinctive context of Shekou, China, and cautioning its wide transferability in discussing the overseas extension of China's development experience.
[13] Wan Y, Zhang L, Xue C Q and Xiao Y (2020) Djibouti: From a colonial fabrication to the deviation of the 'Shekou model'. *Cities*, 97. https://doi.org/10.1016/j.cities.2019.102488.
[14] Port od Djibouti (n.d.) *History of Djibouti Port*. Available at: http://www.portdedjibouti.com/port-history/.

China has gradually expanded its ties with Djibouti since the establishment of their diplomatic relations in 1979. Earlier on China had provided several aid projects to Djibouti, including the construction of the People's Palace of Djibouti in 1985 and the Djibouti National Stadium in 1993.[15] Despite these politically symbolic projects, the bilateral relationship was limited until the early 2000s when China began anti-piracy controls and engaged in maritime logistics by docking a growing number of ships at Djibouti Port. China and Djibouti entered the most recent and strongest phase of their relationship in 2012 when China, Ethiopia and Djibouti agreed to fund the renovation of the derelict Ethio-Djibouti Railway and construct associated port facilities in Djibouti.[16]

Unlike the official inter-state cooperation in earlier times, China's new engagement with Djibouti began to feature and give a central role to the state-owned conglomerate CMG, which developed the Shekou terminal and zone in 1979. In 2013, the Djibouti government sold 23.5% of its stake in the Doraleh Container Terminal, the most important asset of Djibouti Port, to CMG's port and logistics arm – China Merchant Port Holdings Co. (CMP),[17] which has become a major international player in port holdings and operation (Figure 4.2). This marked the official beginning of CMP's introduction and implementation of the PPC mode of development in Djibouti City (Figure 4.3). Similar to both the China–Europe Freight Train (CEFT) and the combined Borten and CLR projects, the Djibouti Port, which was in motion before 2013, has since joined and benefited from the BRI in pushing forward its PPC development.

Figure 4.2 China Merchant Port's global network

Source: www.beltandroad.news. Available online at: https://www.beltandroad.news/2020/03/31/china-merchant-port-holdings-reports-15-4-profits/

In its original, indigenous version of PPC in Shekou, CMG first built a port terminal at the front (facing the sea), followed by an industrial park in the middle (behind the port) and subsequently a new city in the rear (behind the park). These three parts constituted a spatially and functionally integrated urban–industrial complex (see the lower right map of Figure 4.3). Li Xiaopeng, President of CMG, said in an exclusive interview with the *China Daily* in 2017: 'We will use our experience in Shekou and adjust the model to local conditions. We will put this model into practice in Djibouti,' which was the first foreign country to receive an adapted mode of PPC development. Li envisioned this approach to help make Djibouti the 'Shekou of

[15] Wan et al. (2020); see Reference 13.
[16] Styan D (2020) China's Maritime Silk Road and small states: Lessons from the case of Djibouti. *Journal of Contemporary China*, 29(122): 191–206.
[17] Coppieters, Antwerpen (2017) *Port of Djibouti to Become 'Shekou of East Africa' According to Chinese Investors*. Coppieters, Antwerpen. Available at: http://www.coppieters.biz/news/2017/4/19/port-of-djibouti-to-become-shekou-of-east-africa-according-to-chinese-investors.

East Africa' as a hub for regional shipping, logistics and trade.[18] With supplementary funding from the Djibouti Port and Free Zone Authority (DPFZA), CMG invested the bulk of US$590 million to build the first phase of the Doraleh Multipurpose Port (DMP) and to expand the existing Doraleh Container Terminal. CMG began to construct the DMP in 2013, inaugurated it in 2017 and completed its first phase in March 2019.

Built away from Djibouti City and the old and limited French Port (Figure 4.3), which can only accommodate 50,000-ton freight ships, the new DMP offers six berths, all of which are capable of receiving 100,000-ton ships. Ultimately the DMP will have 15 berths spread over four terminals for container, bulk, break bulk and roll on–roll off cargoes. The port can accommodate some of the world's largest container ships with a draught of 16–18 m. The income of the local workforce involved in the port project grew steadily at 8% per year. CMG also invested US$2 million in providing training opportunities for local staff during a three-year span.[19] For the first half of 2018, the DMP handled a container throughput of 450,000 20 foot-equivalent units (TEUs), up by 11.1% year on year, and a bulk cargo volume of 2.87 million tons, up by 23.4% year on year, mainly attributed to the increasing import demand for raw materials driven by the small-scale infrastructure projects in Ethiopia.[20]

To follow through on Shekou's experience with PPC, CMG went through several steps in developing a free-trade zone (FTZ) near the DMP. After signing an agreement with the DPFZA on the FTZ's framework in 2015, CMG brought in the Port of Dalian and IZP, a leading Chinese company specialised in internet cross-border trade and big data, as additional partners. All the partners signed the final agreement to establish the Djibouti International FTZ (DIFTZ) on 15 January 2017, followed by the ground-breaking ceremony. CMG through CMP and its strong investment and construction subsidiaries has invested US$400 million for planning and building the DIFTZ to cover 48.2 km^2 upon eventual completion, which will make it the largest FTZ in Africa. The first phase would occupy an area of 6 km^2 involving US$4 million in investment and including a pilot zone of 2.4 km^2 divided into a trade and logistics subzone and an export-processing subzone (Figure 4.3).

Planned future functions for the zones include financial services, duty-free shopping, automobile assembly and hospitality. With the completion of the basic infrastructure for the small pilot zone, the DIFTZ was inaugurated on 5 July 2018. Attending the ceremony were several heads of state, including the President of Rwanda and Chairperson of the African Union; the President of Sudan; the President of Somalia; the Prime Minister of Ethiopia; and the Chairperson of the African Union Commission. The DIFTZ offers such incentives as 0% corporate and individual income taxes relative to 20% and 18–30% outside the zone. The zone secured realised and intended investments from 78 companies by the end of 2019 and won the award for 'Top 10 Best FTZs 2019' sponsored by *FDI* magazine. The DIFTZ is projected to create around 6000 jobs when the pilot zone is fully completed and 50,000 jobs in 2025, and US$2.5 billion in gross output in 2035.[21]

---

[18] *China Daily* (2017) CMG wants to make African port of Djibouti 'new Shekou'. *China Daily*, 7 March. Available at: https://www.chinadaily.com.cn/business/2017-03/07/content_28455386.htm.
[19] Wan et al. (2020); see Reference 13.
[20] China Merchant Port Holdings Co. (CMP) (2019) *We Connect the World*. Interim Report 2019. Shenzhen: CMP.
[21] Djibouti International Free Trade Zone (DIFTZ) (2019) *The DIFTZ Marketing Plan*, December. Djibouti: DIFTZ.

Figure 4.3   The port–park–city (PPC) mode of development: from Shekou to Djibouti

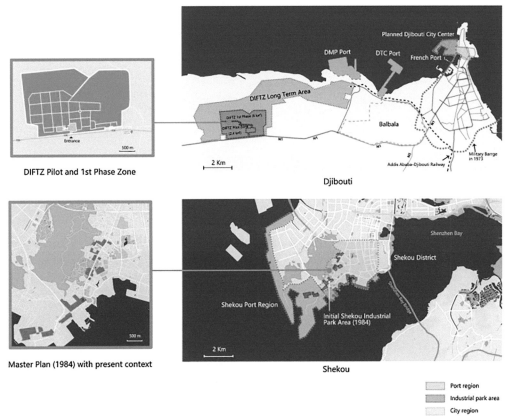

DIFTZ Pilot and 1st Phase Zone

Djibouti

Master Plan (1984) with present context

Shekou

Port region

Industrial park area

City region

Source: Wan Y, Zhang L, Xue C Q and Xiao Y (2020) Djibouti: From a colonial fabrication to the deviation of the 'Shekou model', *Cities*, 97. doi.org/10.1016/j.cities.2019.102488, with permission

Most recently, in July 2020, the Qianhai Shekou FTZ and DIFTZ strengthened their 'teacher–student' or originator–adopter bond through a joint promotion of their investment environments and opportunities (Figure 4.4). In August 2020, the DIFTZ joined a new SEZ free-trade innovation alliance, launched by the Qianhai Shekou FTZ. The alliance includes several SEZs within China, the SDZ in Vientiane, Laos (see chapter 3), the Eastern Industrial Zone in Ethiopia (see below) and seven other China-affiliated overseas SEZs.[22] Except for the zone in Ethiopia, CMG (and CMP), rooted in and expanding from Shekou, Shenzhen, is the common denominator of and driver behind this China-fuelled global SEZ alliance. This also reflects another mode of policy mobility in SEZ development from China to Southeast Asia.[23]

[22]Hambantota Port WeChat Platform (2020) *Hambantota Port Industrial Park Joins the New SEZ Free Trade Innovation Alliance*. Hambantota Port WeChat Platform, 31 August. Available at: https://mp.weixin. qq.com/s/8Uh4_GhLL8HzVMMD4iek0g.

[23]Song T, Liu W, Liu Z and Yeerken W (2018) Chinese overseas industrial parks in Southeast Asia: An examination of policy mobility from the perspective of embeddedness. *Journal of Geography Science*, 28(9): 1288–1306.

The DIFTZ is integral to PPC as the second or middle stage and segment of sequenced development led by port construction or renovation. While the DIFTZ is still at an early stage of development, CMG is already looking ahead to build a new business district with commercial, office and tourism facilities as the old facilities of French Port gradually move to the new DMP (Figure 4.3). This represents city-building or 'C' in the PPC, which focuses on rebuilding the core of Djibouti City and completing by the end of 2021. In trying to localise the full package of PPC, however, CMG faces multiple challenges in the Djibouti national and local contexts that differ considerably from Shekou in China.

Figure 4.4   The Shekou–Djibouti FTZ Alliance.

Source: The Djibouti FTZ WeChat public platform, with permission

The PPC bundle in Shekou comprised 'port in the front, park in the middle, and city in the back' in a fully integrated fashion. In Djibouti City, the PPC under development is spatially fragmented along the coastline (cf. the maps in Figure 4.3). This key difference, in conjunction with Djibouti City's small size and segregated landscape, severely limits its role in stimulating a large national hinterland. Despite also being very small at the outset, Shekou not only grew quickly through spatial integration and economic spillovers but also as an absorbed area of the fast-developing Shenzhen SEZ around it. In addition, Shekou benefited from the complementary inputs from multiple stakeholders led by CMG and supported by the state and nearby Hong Kong, which provided needed initial electricity supply across the border. Djibouti's port and zone have, however, been led and constrained by state monopolies.[24] While Shenzhen was a model for zonal and urban development inside China,[25] this case exposes the limits to transferring a successful mode of development across very different national and local contexts and an inherent challenge to general cross-border policy mobility.

Similar to and different from Haicheng, the private builder of the Borten new city, CMG's dominant role in developing Djibouti Port and DIFTZ reflects its mission to be a major corporate player in the BRI, albeit as a much more powerful SOE. Unlike Haicheng, CMG has shown to be capable of doing more in its partnership with Djibouti. As COVID-19 was about to hit Africa harder, CMG delivered needed medical supplies using its established shipping routes from Shenzhen to Djibouti and organised virtual seminars for experienced Chinese doctors to share valuable information about testing, tracing and clinical care. This represents a kind of knowledge transfer that is critical to economic and social development.

---

[24]Wan et al. (2020); see Reference 13.
[25]O'Donnell M A, Wong W and Bach J (eds.) (2017) *Learning from Shenzhen: China's Post-Mao Experiment from Special Zone to Model City.* Chicago: University of Chicago Press.

4.3.2 China-driven zone-centric mode of development in Ethiopia

If the PPC is key to understanding the influence of Shekou's (Shenzhen, China) development in Djibouti, a different and less complete version of the PPC brings up a sharp lens for examining China's impact on landlocked Ethiopia, which is connected to Djibouti through the new ADR. Even though China's heavy engagement with both countries has brought them closer together, Ethiopia differs drastically from Djibouti along several key dimensions with central importance to our analysis.

With around 110 million people, Ethiopia is Africa's second most populous country, behind only Nigeria, with one of the lowest income per capita in the world (see Appendix A). Only about 20% of Ethiopia's population lives in urban areas. With a median age of 25 years, Ethiopia has a very young population, 53% of which is in the working-age group of 15–64 years.[26] Moreover, Ethiopia's labour cost has been very low, with unit labour cost in making leather shoes being only one-third of Vietnam's and one-fifth of China's or even less. In the meantime, manufacturing only accounted for 4% of Ethiopia's gross domestic product (GDP) during 2008–10.[27] Based on these comparative advantages, Ethiopia has pursued committed industrialisation in recent years, especially through its Second Growth and Transformation Plan for using aggressive measures for rapid industrialisation and structural transformation and becoming a lower-middle income country by 2025. This plan set an ambitious goal of raising the manufacturing sector's share of GDP from 4% to 17% by 2025[28] and led the Ethiopian government to embrace SEZs as the main industrialisation strategy.

By prioritising SEZs, Ethiopia became a leader among African countries who also saw the value in adopting SEZs in the mid-2000s. This broader regional interest was met and formalised in the Overseas Trade and Economic Cooperation Zone (OTECZ) programme during the Third Forum on China–Africa Cooperation in 2006. The programme led China's ministries, banks and enterprises to support the construction and management of six SEZs in five African countries. This created a new private–public partnership in Ethiopia's SEZ development. The Eastern Industrial Zone (EIZ), the first private SEZ in Ethiopia built by private companies from the Zhangjiagang Free Trade Zone in Jiangsu province, received approved as an official OTECZ by the Chinese Ministry of Finance and Ministry of Commerce in 2015.[29] From a private–public vantage point, the EIZ is the first zone for our analysis for how it reflects China's impact on Ethiopia's national and local development.

---

[26]Statista (2020) *China's Share of Global Gross Domestic Product*. Available online at: www.statista.com/statistics/270439/chinas-share-of-global-gross-domestic-product-gdp/.

[27]SIRPA (2017) *Development and Industrialization in Ethiopia: Reflections from China's Experience*. Fudan SIRPA Think Tank Report Series. Shanghai: Fudan University.

[28]Fei D (2018) *Work, Employment, and Training through Africa–China Cooperation Zones: Evidence from the Eastern Industrial Zone in Ethiopia*. Working Paper No. 2018/19. Washington, DC: China Africa Research Initiative, School of Advanced International Studies, Johns Hopkins University, Washington. Available online at: www.sais-cari.org/publications.

[29]Fei (2018); see Reference 28.

https://doi.org/10.1080/2578711X.2020.1823715

The EIZ is located 35 km south-east of Addis Ababa in the town of Dukem, along the Addis Ababa–Djibouti highway to Djibouti Port and the ADR that went into operation on 1 January 2018. This favourable location, coupled with being Ethiopia's first SEZ, attracted foreign investors early including Chinese companies. The resident companies included mainly those in textiles, footwear, automobile assembly and construction materials. In 2011, Huajian Group, a large private shoe company based in the southern Chinese city of Dongguan, opened a factory in the EIZ and began producing footwear for large and famous international companies and brands such as Guess and Naturaliser.

Politically connected to the top Chinese leadership and personally linked to a former Ethiopian Prime Minister, the founder and Chairman of Huajian Group Zhang Ronghua created the creating Huajian International Shoe City (Ethiopia) in the EIZ as an effort to help promote China–Africa economic cooperation. Zhang's patriotic interest converged with Huajian's business goals and capacities as one of China's largest makers of leather women's shoes for the European and US markets. First, he saw the very low labour costs, as low as 10% of the rising manufacturing wages in China, as a significant comparative advantage, while local productivity could reach 60% of Chinese workers. An improvement to 80% would allow Huajian to make a 15% profit,[30] whereas the profit margin for labour-intensive industries such as shoes in China had already fallen to around 3–5%. Second, a top leather-supplying country in the world, Ethiopia generates 1.4 million pieces of cow leather, 1.7 million pieces of goat leather and 1.3 million pieces of sheep leather annually. A leather-processing company from India, which is known for quality leather processing, supplies 400,000 m^2 of leather to, and earns 33% of its revenue from, just Huajian, which has developed around 60 suppliers in Ethiopia.[31] Third, Ethiopia can send tariff-free exports to North America and Europe, while China no longer enjoys low wages and tariff-free exports.[32]

To start out, Huajian brought over 300 Chinese expatriates in different operations of shoe production from Dongguan to work with and train a few hundred local workers. The Chinese expatriates also included student trainees from a Huajian-owned shoe-making school in China. At peak employment in 2015, there were six production lines attended by over 4000 workers.[33] As of 2016, Huajian employed around 4600 local workers, of which only 2400 worked on shifts in two workshops (Figure 4.5), while the Chinese expatriates dropped in number to about 160. According to a 2016 survey, of 204 workers in the EIZ including 114

---

[30]A reporter's interview with Zhang Ronghua, Chairman of Huajian Group, on Caijing TV, May 2017, re-aired on the AfricanBusiness WeChat public platform, 6 September 2020. Available at: https://mp.weixin.qq.com/s/6HmxnlTXJ7lvmOPRtWTabA.

[31]A reporter's interview with Zhang Yunqi, daughter of Zhang Ronghua and a Vice-General Manager of Huajian Group, on a Guangdong province television station, 2017; re-aired on the AfricanBusiness WeChat public platform, 7 September 2020. Available at: https://mp.weixin.qq.com/s/NQjVLvTBG3o1CdXYC8V_ow.

[32]Chen X (2020) From follower to leader: China's development of special economic zones and its global significance. *European Financial Review*, December–January: 22–29.

[33]Lead author's interview with a Chinese shoe-making professional who was a worker at Huajian (Ethiopia) during 2012–15.

in footwear, mostly working at Huajian, the average workers earned about US$97 monthly, higher than the national average of US$49, while Ethiopian workers who could speak Chinese and English besides their native tongue could earn as much as US$400 a month.[34] The surveyed workers rated 3.9 (on a 0–5 scale) on the question of 'the Chinese are competent in their professional skills', 3.4 on 'on-the-job training in the company is helpful to improve your skills' and only 2.8 on 'the Chinese company often provides on-the-job training to you'.[35] Huajian also brought a selected number of Ethiopian workers

Figure 4.5   A Huajian shoe factory in Ethiopia

Source: Huajian Group archival photograph, with permission

to China for training. This case indicates that one private Chinese company in one SEZ began to matter in creating many jobs at a competitive local wage scale with some training.

While its very first factory in the EIZ was taking off in January 2012, Huajian signed a memorandum of understanding (MOU) with the Ethiopian government to build the 'Ethio-China Light Industrial City' near Addis Ababa. Also known as the Huajian Light Industrial City, the large-scale and integrated project not only focuses on light manufacturing but also includes trade, services and associated residential functions in a broader urban environment. While this project is narrower than Borten, Huajian is similar to Haicheng, the builder of Borten (see chapter 3), as both are private Chinese companies that have gone beyond manufacturing and real estate in building integrated infrastructure projects. With a total investment of US$1 billion, the zone/city is planned to cover 138 hectares and a built area of 1.5 million m^2 in factory buildings and other auxiliary facilities and basic infrastructure upon completion in 2020. It is expected to create 50,000–60,000 jobs and earn US$2 billion in foreign exchange, as the flagship platform for China-assisted industrialisation in Africa.[36] While the official ceremony for ground-breaking was not held until April 2016, construction has proceeded sufficiently that three production lines are currently in operation employing only about 800 workers, falling short of the scheduled completion and targeted total employment. With the experience working with Chinese workers and financial security from their employment at the Huajian factory, four young Ethiopian workers are planning to start a garment workshop of their own in the near future.[37] Now part of the a new SEZ alliance launched by China (see above), the EIZ together with the Huanjian Light Industrial City are expected to further strengthen China–Ethiopia manufacturing and trade links through a powerful SOE such as CMG and a large private company such as Huajian.

[34]SIRPA (2017); see Reference 27.

[35]Fei (2018); see Reference 28.

[36]Huajian Group (2019) *Huajian in Africa, A Promotional Booklet*. Huajian Group.

[37]Xinhua (2019) *Young Ethiopians Find Career Opportunities at Chinese Firms*. Xinhua, 30 June. Available at: www.xinhuanet.com/english/2019-06/30/c_138186698.htm.

Through its factories, Huajian has created multiple local opportunities for speeding up Ethiopia's development through labour-intensive industrialisation. This has created jobs and its extended benefit in the accumulation of experience and training through Chinese expatriates working on-site and Ethiopian workers going to China. As of June 2020, Huajian's total employment in Ethiopia remained around 3500. In building its larger Light Industrial City, Huajian has also added a church and a mosque where Ethiopian workers can have respective religious services.[38]

As Huajian has deepened its economic involvement in Ethiopia, it has begun to expand into other parts of Africa. In April 2019, Huajian Group announced that it would invest heavily in the new Roubiki Leather City on the outskirts of Cairo. While leather linked Ethiopia to Egypt, Huajian's Chairman Zhang revealed that his group's plan to invest in Egypt fit with the framework of the BRI with Egypt as a focal point for Africa.[39]

Similar to the private company Haicheng, which has built the Borten new zone/city project on the China–Laos border as part of the BRI (see chapter 3), Huajian has been more vocal and active in supporting the BRI, even though it entry into Ethiopia in 2011 as a private investor predated the BRI's onset in 2013. Moreover, in the spirit of supporting China–Africa cooperation in fighting COVID-19, Huajian created a new subsidiary, Huajian Medical Technology Co., on 26 March 2020. Using this vehicle, Huajian made and donated 1.2 million masks to 11 African countries, including Ethiopia (Figure 4.6), ramping up its engagement with Africa through a play of overseas corporate social responsibility.

Figure 4.6   Huajian donating medical supplies to Ethiopia

Source: Huajian Group archival photograph, with permission

Besides Huajian, Alibaba is a much larger and more powerful private company that has combined its involvement in Africa in support of the BRI with its recent effort to help Africa fight the pandemic. Alibaba has led the Electronic World Trade Platform, with Ethiopia as a partner and Rwanda as a hub, to create a more inclusive digital global economy. It fits with the mission and implementation of the DSR in offering and expanding digitally enabled service economy in Africa that complements its manufacturing development. To help further this digital initiative, in March 2020, the Jack Ma Foundation and Alibaba Foundation announced to donate 500 ventilators, 200,000 suits and face shields, 2000 thermometers, 1 million swabs and extraction kits, and 500,000 gloves to Africa using Addis Ababa as a distribution hub.[40] These efforts

---

[38]Lead author's interview with a Chinese shoe-making professional; see Reference 33.

[39]Xinhua (2019) *China's Giant Shoe Manufacturer Huajian to Pump Investments in Egypt: Minister*. Xinhua, 11 April. Available at: http://www.xinhuanet.com/english/2019-04/11/c_137966305.htm.

[40]Dorothy So (2020) *Jack Ma Foundation Equips Africa in Fight against Coronavirus*. Dorothy So, 17 March. Available at: https://www.alizila.com/jack-ma-foundation-equips-africa-in-fight-against-covid-19/.

represent a somewhat coordinated Chinese approach to fostering broad development in Ethiopia, and Africa more broadly, through both public and private channels with their resources.

4.3.3 Unlocking landlocked exports through the Addis Ababa–Djibouti Railway

The two Huajian factories in both the EIZ and the newer light industrial city churned out 5 million pairs of shoes for export every year, earning US$31 million in foreign exchange for Ethiopia in 2017 alone.[41] During the 2018–19 fiscal year, Ethiopia earned US$142 million in exports, 50% higher than the previous year,[42] from all China-built and managed industrial parks, including the Jimma Industrial Park in western Ethiopia that Huajian agreed to operate in 2019. Both the Ethiopia–Djibouti highway and the ADR transport these Ethiopian exports, 90% of which go through Djibouti that depends on Ethiopia for 70% of its port activities. The latter can go from Addis Ababa to Djibouti within 11 hours, while it would take three days for trucks. The freight line is capable of transporting 106 containers in a single route and currently runs twice a day in each direction. The freight service aims to transport 85% of national freighter facility by taking over 40–50% of what is now being carried by trucks.[43] This includes transporting different kinds of freight services including picking up and dropping off perishable goods, vehicles, cereals and fertilisers at Indode, Mojo and Adama stations (Figure 4.1).

The ADR's total railway capacity is 24.9 million tonnes of freight annually, with 6 million tonnes annually expected in 2023. This target is linked to the upgrading works at the Port of Doraleh to expand its annual cargo handling capacity from 6 to 14 million tonnes, with the aim of reaching 10 million tonnes of cargo by 2022.[44] Thus far, the ADR freight line has not fully lived up to its expected capacity for different reasons. Electricity shortages have sometimes slowed the train, which has to stop if it runs into camels or other wild animals crossing the tracks. Trains in either direction must be scheduled at long intervals due to the absence of easy bypassing points along the way. As a positive, Chinese engineers have trained Ethiopian drivers to operate both the freight and passenger train services as a forward-looking effort to make the ADR more sustainable. Regionally, the signing of a peace treaty in July 2019 between Ethiopia and Eritrea provided Ethiopia access to such Eritrean ports as Assab (Figure 4.1), as Djibouti Port had been Ethiopia's sole access to the sea. Nevertheless, as China-built and Ethiopian industrial zones, mostly located close to the railway, produce more exports, it will generate more freight cargo for the ADR as expected from Borten and the SDZ for the CLR (see chapter 3). This calls for the Ethiopian government to loosen its monopoly over both the rail and highway operations to allow competitive pricing and a more complementary use of either mode of transportation.

---

[41] Xinhua (2019) *Chinese Firm Signs Agreement to Manage Ethiopian Industrial Park*. Xinhua, 31 May. Available at: http://www.xinhuanet.com/english/2019-05/31/c_138103636.htm.

[42] *Global Times* (2019) Chinese-built industrial parks help boost Ethiopian exports. *Global Times*, 10 August. Available at: http://www.globaltimes.cn/content/1160926.shtml.

[43] Reported on https://www.ena.et/en/?p=8779.

[44] Wikipedia (n.d.) Addis Ababa–Djibouti Railway (ADR). Available at: https://en.wikipedia.org/wiki/Addis_Ababa%E2%80%93Djibouti_Railway.

4.4 SUMMARY AND POLICY RECOMMENDATIONS

Urbanisation has stimulated and sustained China's economic development through rapid and expansive industrial production that originated from and spread beyond its first few SEZs near seaports in southern China. Embodied by Shekou and Shenzhen, this mode of development features the spatial integration of PPC layouts and functions. Based on its original PPC project in Shekou in 1979, the state-owned CMG has 'exported' the modified the PPC mode to a few other countries, starting with Djibouti. We have shown that an adapted version of the PPC in Djibouti Port and Djibouti City has led to partial success due to inherent barriers in the local context. China-linked SEZs in Ethiopia, built and operated primarily by a private company (Huajian), have created many jobs, offered some training and generated many exports. While the ADR has created a new transport corridor between Ethiopia's exports and Djibouti Port, it has not reached its targeted carrying capacity for lack of sufficient cargo, continued competition from trucking and inefficient state management.

Relative to its impacts on globalisation and urbanisation, the BRI faces more constraints on its capacity of sustaining a positive effect on economic development with reference to the UN's SDGs, especially through and after the COVID-19 pandemic. The UN has recently projected that the pandemic is likely to push 40–60 million people back into extreme poverty, causing the first increase in global poverty in more than 20 years.[45] As the Chinese economy has contracted 6.8% in the first quarter of 2020 and 3.0% for the year, several least developed African countries such as Angola, Democratic Republic of Congo, Ethiopia, Eritrea and South Sudan (see Appendix A) will suffer heavily due to their 40% plus export dependence on China, especially for their commodities such as oil. Africa's development will take a second hit from declined investment by China as the continent's largest investor.[46]

If African countries have to borrow more to finance their fight against the pandemic and recovery from it, it will worsen their heavy national debts whose ratio to GDP rose from an average of 37% in 2012 to 59% in 2019.[47] Djibouti is a worst-case scenario as its debt-to-GDP ratio is around 80%, a good portion of which is owed to China. Laos is also among the most indebted to China due to its very heavy borrowing for the CLR (Figure 4.7). However, it is not realistic for small countries such as Djibouti and Laos to develop major port or rail projects without taking the risk in large external financing.[48] In few less and least developed countries, the heavy debts owed to China have developed as their leaders pursued their own development agendas

---

[45] United Nations (2020) *Progress towards the Sustainable Development Goals*. Report of the Secretary-General. New York: United Nations General Assembly.

[46] Organisation for Economic Co-operation and Development (OECD) (2020) *COVID-19 and Africa: Socio-Economic Implications and Policy Responses*. Report. Available at: http://www.oecd.org/coronavirus/policy-responses/covid-19-and-africa-socio-economic-implications-and-policy-responses-96e1b282/.

[47] Brookings Institution (2020) Figures of the week: The macroeconomic impact of COVID-19 in Africa. In *Africa in Focus*. Washington, DC: Brookings Institution. Available at: https://www.brookings.edu/blog/africa-in-focus/2020/04/16/figures-of-the-week-the-macroeconomic-impact-of-covid-19-in-africa/.

[48] Bautigam D (2020) A critical look at Chinese 'debt-trap diplomacy': The rise of a meme. *Area Development and Policy*, 5(1): 1–14.

and vested interests at regional or local levels, such as Sri Lanka.[49] Nevertheless, China is fully aware of the Western rhetoric about debt diplomacy and the real danger in debt default, worsened by the coronavirus in 2020. It has recently suspended some debt repayments for 77 developing countries and regions as part of the G20 debt relief initiative to help impoverished countries weather economic difficulties amid the coronavirus pandemic. Against these headwinds, we recommend policies to international and Chinese policy-makers who work in the broad area of development as it pertains to the BRI (Box 4.1).

Figure 4.7   Eight heavily indebted developing countries due to some BRI borrowing

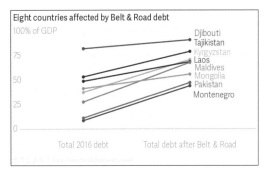

Source: Center for Global Development chart, with permission

Box 4.1   Policy recommendations for the BRI versus development:

- We encourage international development agencies and donors to work more cooperatively with China in conducting careful and transparent risk assessments for development-oriented BRI projects in the future. A multilateral approach will invoke more trust and transparency from less and least developed BRI partner countries in receiving development projects from China
- We recommend policies for both China and African countries to send and receive labour-intensive manufacturing investment, full linking and integrating rising production costs in China, and lower production costs in Africa. This policy not only can benefit from the available factory spaces in the special economic zones (SEZs) built and operated by China, but also further lessen Africa's dependency on commodity exports that have not brought sufficient and sustainable development
- We propose policies to incentivise a larger number of private Chinese companies such as Huajian and state-owned enterprises (SOEs) to move more extended production facilities in sunset industries to Africa and build more complete supply chains locally as the leather shoe industry in Ethiopia. These policies can be coordinated with European and American multinational companies that own brands in and manage supply chains and import finished products from these industries (see chapter 4).
- We recommend continued on-the-job training and skill development at China-invested factories in developing countries with great manufacturing and export potentials such as Ethiopia as an effective and sustainable way of scaling and spreading the most crucial element of catch-up development
- There should be more effective and customised ways of delivering the port–park–city (PPC) bundle of development to more countries besides Djibouti. While port construction and upgrading leads the process and sequence of development where it applies, it is more practical to use SEZs to jumpstart manufacturing and then diversity and expand them into more integrated and comprehensive urban

---

[49] Jones L and Hameiri S (2020) *Debunking the Myth of 'Debt-Trap Diplomacy': How Recipient Countries Shape China's Belt and Road Initiative*. Research Paper, August. London: Chatham House.

economic development. This flexible application of PPC reflects the combination and cross-over between the cases in chapters 3 and 4

- We recommend that China strengthen an integrated focus on social and health development to benefit the poorest countries, especially those in the low-income category (see Appendix A) that have suffered from negative consequences of COVID-19. Building on China's past and generally welcome practice of sending medical teams to poor developing countries, this renewed social development focus should elevate the targeted improvement of healthcare capacities and facilities to nourish a more healthy workforce for accelerated and sustainable economic development

5. A SYNTHESIS AND LOOKING FORWARD

5.1 INTRODUCTION

We anchor this book to a bold statement that the BRI has ushered in an era of epochal regionalisation. We have taken this statement further into a more ambitious argument that the BRI's regionalising dynamics are reshaping globalisation, urbanisation and development simultaneously and relationally. Driven by globalisation from above and pushed by urbanisation and development from below, the BRI has taken on an increasingly crucial middling role in bridging and integrating global, national and local economies. In our framework (Figure 1.5), we see the BRI as new regionalisation that triangulates three large-scale and powerful processes of globalisation, urbanisation and development.

5.2 FROM A SINGLE INITIATIVE TO A SYNERGISTIC FORCE

While proposed as a single initiative, the BRI carries China's ambitious and broad vision and goals for both itself and the world (for Xi Jinping's speech, see Box 5.1). How does the BRI move from a single initiative launched by one powerful country to a synergistic force that can deliver on all its stated ideals and goals involving many other countries? This calls for the BRI to create connected mechanisms to produce shared positive and lasting impacts. We have uncovered the BRI's key mechanisms as cross-border connectivities for globalisation, embedded and relational infrastructures for urbanisation, and sustainable ways of development. They are instrumental in bringing the varied geographies and projects of the BRI to connect through its regional corridors with sustained impacts.

> **Box 5.1   China's President Xi Jinping's summary of the BRI:**
>
> China will actively promote international co-operation through the Belt and Road Initiative. In doing so, we hope to achieve policy, infrastructure, trade, financial, and people-to-people connectivity and thus build a new platform for international co-operation to create new drivers of shared development.
>
> Speech delivered at the 19th National Congress of the Communist Party of China, 18 October 2017

We have captured part of the BRI's synergistic force through three case studies. First, the cases take the shape of land-based economic and transport corridors. They have stimulated opportunities for landlocked developing countries (Central Asia, Laos and Ethiopia) to create broader cross-border links and a more direct access to the sea and maritime trade. Second, they involve new China-built or orchestrated freight (and passenger) railways – China–Europe Freight Train (CEFT), China–Laos Railway (CLR) and Addis Ababa–Djibouti Railway (ADR) – that link marginal and underdeveloped cities and regions over long distances. Third, this long-distance connectivity is accompanied and reinforced by the construction of localised urban infrastructure such as new cities and special economic zones (SEZs) in Laos, Djibouti and Ethiopia. They amount to converged efforts by several less and least developed countries to capitalise on globalisation, urbanisation and development through the BRI.

https://doi.org/10.1080/2578711X.2020.1823717

The three cases also show that the BRI features the joint participation of both Chinese state-owned and private companies and an unplanned division of labour between them. It debunks the prevailing notion that the BRI is China's one-state initiative to gain global geopolitical influence. Moreover, with comparative advantages and disadvantages in scale and financing power relative to flexibility and special expertise, large state-owned enterprises (SOEs) and smaller private companies have produced some synergy and thus contributed the BRI's broader impact on globalisation, urbanisation and development. To further synergise the actors and actions in our case studies, we distil the essential elements of the policy recommendations for each of the three domains and summarise them in Table 5.1.

Table 5.1   The BRI's impacts on globalisation, urbanisation and development and recommended policy responses.:

BRI's impacts	Positive/beneficial	Challenging/ questionable	Recommended policy responses
Globalisation • Benefits and tensions • Deglobalisation and nationalism • Stronger regionalisation • Leadership shift	• Keeping openness • Creating new corridors of connectivity • Facilitating greater trade • Offering new leadership	• Geopolitical threat • Lack of multilateralism • Potential ideological division • Undue Chinese influence	• Recognising BRI's significance • Creating cross-border cooperation • Prioritising the logistics sector • Incentivising and encouraging Western firms to participate
Urbanisation • Accelerating in Asia and Africa • Infrastructure deficits • Lagging and neglected peripheral cities	• Constructing new cities • Providing embedded infrastructure • Building inter-city transport links	• Land grab • Environmental impact • Reinforcing spatial disparities • Wasteful infrastructure investment	• Better government coordination • More realistic planning • More vigilant about environment • Strengthening local governance
Development • Multidimensional and unequal • Landlocked problem • Catch-up process • Sustainability challenges	• Forging land–sea connections • Building industrial zones • Creating jobs • Offering skill training	• Relocating polluting industries • Insufficient local employment • Suspect labour practices • Lagging social development	• Avoiding the debt trap and offering select debt relief • More manufacturing transfer • Enhancing training and localisation

Source: Lead author.

5.3   CAN THE BRI BECOME A REGIONAL AND A GLOBAL PUBLIC GOOD?

As we bring the book to a close, we raise a challenging long-run question of whether the BRI, while already impactful in the three areas of our study, can become a regional public good (RPG) capable of generating more positive benefits commensurate with the scale and length of the corridors. In connection and extension, can the BRI even scale up from an RPG to a global public good (GPG) that spreads the BRI's synergistic impact beyond the regional corridors and international boundaries they traverse? While an RPG can refer to the management of a river basin, GPGs are public goods with benefits and costs such as climate change, public health, financial stability and knowledge production that extend across countries and regions in an open and inclusive manner.[1] The BRI has already touched upon and impacted some of these public goods at a regional scale, as revealed by our three case studies. It has the potential to become a real RPG, if not a potential GPG, over time given how it has played out on the ground.

First, beyond the generally perceived geographical sweeping scope, the BRI's broad strength lies in a narrower band of new cross-border regional economic terrains defined and shaped by several growth corridors and a score of sub-corridors. They feature CEFT routes across the vast Eurasia, China-built new cities and SEZs linked by the CLR across the China–Southeast Asia borderlands and new sea–land manufacturing and transport connections via the ADR between Djibouti and Ethiopia in the Horn of Africa. Without these new cross-border regional connections spun by the BRI, some of the subnational units such as cities and their neighbouring areas would not have emerged from less familiar and more marginal corners of the world onto the global stage. They exemplify the BRI's new regionalising impacts on globalisation, urbanisation and development. If these impacts can become more multiplicative as they extend and intersect across more regions and cities on both sides of multiple international boundaries (Table 5.1), they would help set and stretch the more open and connected geographical parameters of the BRI serving as multiple RPGs.

As the COVID-19 pandemic has reset the globalisation debate by moving deglobalisation to the forefront, the BRI stands as a potential GPG that can steer the debate toward the potential new benefits of a China-led globalisation by sustaining a continued open stance through promoting trade flows and infrastructure connections, even against the severe disruption of the pandemic. With its many large-scale infrastructure projects already localised and spreading beyond localities, the BRI poses major challenges to its projects' immediate and adjacent biophysical environments, especially if some of these projects end up being badly managed and thus unsustainable. This exposes the potential downside of the BRI as a potential GPG, despite its stated intentions to do good regionally and globally. The policy recommendations we have put forth can help mitigate potential risks carried and projected by the BRI regarding its long-term viability and broader acceptance.

Finally, by exerting China's inside-out impacts on globalisation, urbanisation and development through its time horizon, the BRI carries a long-run inertia and dynamic that may outlast the pandemic's shorter run impact on the global economy. The BRI's future impact hinges on both China's domestic restructuring through the pandemic and its spillover effects from the China-built overseas infrastructure. As China turns more to domestic consumption to sustain its recovery from COVID-19 and post-COVID-19 growth in the face of slow and weak global recovery, through its new implemented Dual Circulation Strategy (DCS), the BRI can ride on the already regionalised and localised infrastructure projects and cross-border connections to foster further global cooperation. Our recommended policies aim to alert all parties and policy-makers with current and future connections to the BRI to what can and should be done to turn this China-driven initiative into a potential GPG.

---

[1] Ersoy B A (2011) *Globalization and Global Public Goods, An Open Access Peer-Reviewed Chapter.* Available online at: https://www.intechopen.com/books/new-knowledge-in-a-new-era-of-globalization/globalization-and-global-public-goods.

APPENDIX A: THE BOTTOM BILLION LAG AND BRI COUNTRIES BY INCOME LEVELS

The bottom billion lag	Countries by income category, 2018	The BRI bridge
*In *The Bottom Billion*, Paul Collier argued that about 1 billion people an around 58 least developing countries had been trapped at the bottom of the development ladder, while 4 billion people in other developing countries had stayed or moved up into the middle-income position such as China, and the remaining 1 billion people lived in the rich world	High Income (*n* = 80): gross national income per capita: ≥ US$12,376: Andorra, *Antigua and Barbuda*, Aruba, Australia, *Austria*, Bahamas, **Bahrain**, *Barbados*, Belgium, Bermuda, British Virgin Islands, **Brunei**, Canada, Cayman Islands, Channel Islands, *Chile*, **Croatia**, Curacao, *Cyprus*, **Czech Republic**, Denmark, **Estonia**, Faroe Islands, Finland, France, French Polynesia, Germany, Gibraltar, <u>Greece</u>, Greenland, Guam, <u>Hong Kong SAR, China</u>, **Hungary**, Iceland, Ireland, Isle of Man, **Israel**, *Italy*, Japan, *South Korea*, **Kuwait**, **Latvia**, Liechtenstein, **Lithuania**, *Luxembourg*, Macao SAR, *Malta*, Monaco, Netherlands, New Caledonia, *New Zealand*, Northern Mariana Islands, Norway, **Oman**, Palau, *Panama*, **Poland**, *Portugal*, Puerto Rico, **Qatar**, San Marino, **Saudi Arabia**, *Seychelles*, **Singapore**, Sint Maarten, **Slovakia**, **Slovenia**, Spain, St Kitts and Nevis, St Martin, Sweden, Switzerland, <u>Taiwan, China</u>, *Trinidad and Tobago*, Turks and Caicos Islands, **United Arab Emirates (UAE)**, UK, USA, *Uruguay* and Virgin Islands	**The BRI can tackle the bottom billion problem by building connective infrastructure to help developing countries trade more, urbanise faster and create more manufacturing. It does so by forging cooperation among countries across the four income categories
While he did not list all 58 countries containing the bottom billion, he mentioned Cambodia, Chad, Ethiopia, Haiti, Laos, Myanmar, Uganda and Yemen as examples		In the high-income category, 19 (23.8%) countries are located on or along the six BRI corridors and referred as BRI corridor countries (shown in bold; World Bank 2019) minus Hong Kong and Taiwan, while 15 (18.8%) other countries have signed BRI cooperation agreements with China (shown in italics), and 43 (53.8%) countries belong to neither group
*While recognising that relatively little Western aid and investment and international development assistance had gone to help the bottom billion, Collier identified four development traps that held the bottom billion in place: (1) chronic conflict, (2) the natural resource curse, (3) landlocked with bad neighbours and (4) bad governance in small countries	Upper middle income (*n* = 60): gross national income per capita: US$3996–US$12,375: **Albania**, *Algeria*, American Samoa, Argentina, **Armenia**, **Azerbaijan**, **Belarus**, Belize, **Bosnia and Herzegovina**, Botswana, Brazil, **Bulgaria**, ***China***, Colombia, *Costa Rica*, *Cuba*, *Dominica*, *Dominican Republic*, *Ecuador*, *Equatorial Guinea*, *Fiji*, *Gabon*, **Georgia**, *Grenada*, Guatemala, *Guyana*, **Iran**, **Iraq**, *Jamaica*, **Jordan**, **Kazakhstan**, Kosovo, **Lebanon**, *Libya*, **Malaysia**, **Maldives**, Marshall Islands, Mauritius, Mexico, **Montenegro**, *Namibia*, Nauru, **North Macedonia**, Paraguay, *Peru*, **Romania**, **Russia**, *Samoa*, **Serbia**, *South Africa*, **Sri Lanka**, St Lucia, St Vincent and Grenadines, *Suriname*, **Thailand**, *Tonga*, **Turkey**, **Turkmenistan**, Tuvalu and *Venezuela*	**China drives the BRI from this income category, which includes countries with comparable income and development as China
		In this income category, 23 (38.3%) are BRI corridor countries except China itself, while 19 (31.6%) have signed BRI cooperation agreements, and 16 (26.7%) others belong to neither

(Continued)

The bottom billion lag	Countries by income category, 2018	The BRI bridge
The combined population of the low-middle-income countries was around 3 billion in 2018	Low-middle income (**n** = 47): gross national income per capita: US$1026–US$3995: *Angola*, **Bangladesh**, **Bhutan**, *Bolivia*, *Cabo Verde*, **Cambodia**, *Cameroon*, *Comoros*, [AQ2] Congo Republic, *Cote d'Ivoire*, Djibouti, **Egypt**, *El Salvador*, Eswatini, *Ghana*, Honduras, **India**, **Indonesia**, Kenya, Kiribati, **Kyrgyzstan**, **Laos**, *Lesotho*, *Mauritania*, *Micronesia*, [AQ3] Federal States, **Moldova**, **Mongolia**, *Morocco*, **Myanmar**, Nicaragua, *Nigeria*, **Pakistan**, *Papua New Guinea*, **Philippines**, Sao Tome and Principe, *Senegal*, *Solomon Islands*, *Sudan*, **Timor-Leste**, *Tunisia*, **Ukraine**, **Uzbekistan**, *Vanuatu*, **Vietnam**, **Palestine**, *Zambia* and *Zimbabwe*	**Complementary to China with lower income and development levels, these countries may cooperate with and benefit from the BRI most effectively
*This category includes several countries that were in the bottom billion stratum such as Cambodia, Laos, Myanmar and Pakistan, which happen to be the most actively engaged BRI countries		This income category contains 20 (42.6%) BRI corridor countries, 21 (44.7%) countries with BRI cooperation agreements and only five (10.6%) that belong to neither
The combined population of the low-income countries was 705 million in 2018	Low income (*n* = 31): gross national income per capita: ≤ US$1025: **Afghanistan**, *Benin*, Burkina Faso, *Burundi*, Central African Republic, *Chad*, *Congo, Democratic Republic*, Eritrea, *Ethiopia*, *Gambia*, *Guinea*, Guinea-Bissau, Haiti, North Korea, *Liberia*, *Madagascar*, Malawi, *Mali*, *Mozambique*, **Nepal**, *Niger*, *Rwanda*, *Sierra Leone*, *Somalia*, *South Sudan*, **Syria**, **Tajikistan**, Tanzania, *Togo*, *Uganda* and **Yemen**	**These poorest have the most to gain from the BRI with the least institutional capacity to cooperate
*This category includes most of the countries in the bottom billion around 2005		This income category has six (19.4%) BRI corridor countries, 18 (58.1%) with cooperation agreements, and only seven (22.6%) that belong to neither

Sources: Lead author's compilation from the Belt and Road Portal (2020). Available online at: https://eng.yidaiyilu.gov. cn/info/iList.jsp?cat_id=10076; World Bank (2019) *Belt and Road Economics: Opportunities and Risks of Transport Corridors*. Washington, DC: World Bank; and other sources.

Note: There is no consistently accurate count of the number of countries that are either officially committed participants in the BRI or have signed a cooperation agreement with China regarding an individual BRI-related project. We underline six of the World Bank's count of 71 countries (shown in bold) that are usually excluded from what China officially defines as BRI countries. We also italicise 70 countries or areas with at least one BRI cooperation agreement. This raises the number of countries connected with the BRI to around 140 across all four categories of income, weighted more to the low-middle- and low-income categories.

REGIONAL STUDIES POLICY IMPACT BOOKS

The Regional Studies Policy Impact books are series of "Expo" publications from the Regional Studies Association. The books in this series are commissioned to address topical policy questions of contemporary importance to all communities engaged in regional and urban studies issues. The term "Expo" is taken to mean "a comprehensive description and meaning of an idea or theory". The publication style uses clear and coherent narrative addressing evidence for different policy and theoretical positions. Each topic is broad in scope, achieving global reach and relevance wherever possible. There is a consistent focus on the impact of policy research both in terms its reach to policy, academic and practitioner communities and also in its significance, to show how evidence can inform policy change within regional and urban studies.

Every place matters: towards effective place-based policy

By Andrew Beer, Fiona McKenzie, Jiří Blažek, Markku Sotarauta & Sarah Ayres (2020)

Across the globe policy makers implement, and academics teach and undertake research upon, place-based policy. But what is place-based policy, what does it aspire to achieve, what are the benefits of place-based approaches relative to other forms of policy, and what are the key determinants of success for this type of government intervention? This Policy Expo examines these questions, reviewing the literature and the experience of places and their governments around the world. We find place-based policies are essential in contemporary economies, providing solutions to otherwise intractable challenges such as the long-term decline of cities and regions. For those working in public sector agencies the success or failure of place-based policies is largely attributable to governance arrangements, but for researchers the community that is the subject of this policy effort, and its leadership, determines outcomes. This Policy Expo explores the differing perspectives on place-based policy and maps out the essential components of effective and impactful actions by government at the scale of individual places.

Revitalising Lagging Regions: Smart Specialisation and Industry 4.0

Edited By Mariachiara Barzotto, Carlo Corradini, Felicia M Fai, Sandrine Labory & Philip R Tomlinson (2019)

This Expo book brings together leading academic and policymaker experts to reflect on the significant challenges faced by lagging regions in participating in the European Union's Research and Innovation Strategies for Smart Specialisation (RIS3) programme. In doing so, the book offers a set of new policy recommendations on the design and implementation of appropriate Smart Specialisation Strategies (S3) in lagging regions, which may enable them to benefit from the opportunities of digitalisation and Industry 4.0 (I4.0).

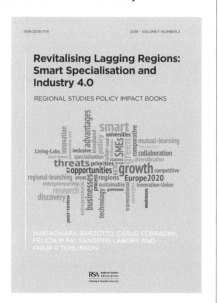

Towards Cohesion Policy 4.0: Structural Transformation and Inclusive Growth

By John Bachtler, Joaquim Oliveira Martins, Peter Wostner and Piotr Zuber (2019)

In the context of the debate on the future of Europe, this book makes the case for a new approach to structural transformation, growth and cohesion in the EU. It explores both the opportunities and challenges from globalisation and technological change, the widening differences in productivity between leading and lagging regions, and the need for a new policy framework capable of delivering inclusive growth.

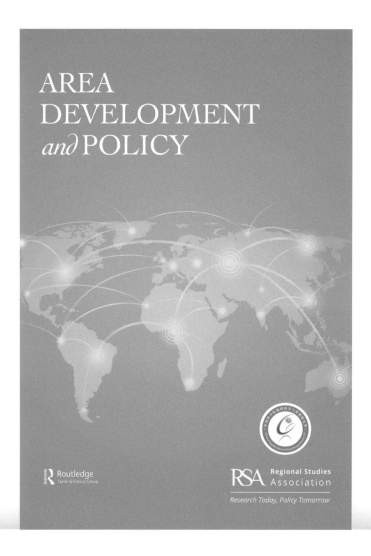
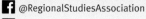